AF512251

aah! Chocolate

SANJEEV KAPOOR

In association with Alyona Kapoor

www.sanjeevkapoor.com

Author's note

What is it about chocolate that fascinates one and all? There are hundreds of adjectives that a chocoholic will use to describe the sweetness of it but for me, chocolate is a journey of discovery! My book AAH! CHOCOLATE is a tribute to all things chocolatey that a home cook can possibly make, create and swoon for in the kitchen. By all means, use this intelligent ingredient in all that you can think of – beverages, cakes, cookies, mousses, moulded titbits, mithais, desserts, garnishes...

My experiments with chocolate have been a work-in-progress. My experiences with chocolate as an ingredient have been soul satisfying. So here is a collection of my superlative experiences that have been put into a good narrative, bordering on the sweet! Each recipe can well be called a story because once you serve the dish at home to your loved ones, family and friends, there are memories that will be indelibly ingrained in their minds. Their hearts will always remember fondly that you gave them something so chocolatey that they wished they'd never stopped eating!

So start up with a comforting mug of Spiced Hot Chocolate. For that grand cake you always wanted to make for your birthday, check out Opera Cake. As brownies rule the roost, take it up a notch higher with Millionaire Chocolate Brownie, make them, gift them as you please. Boss coming over for dinner? Impress with Chocolate Mille Feuille. Those who are born with sticky jaws with not just one sweet tooth, then Caramel Centered Chocolate will be perfect. For any forthcoming festival, gift packs of Chocolate Paan to your loved ones. For the passionate baker, there is a milieu of cookies and treats like Chocolate Shrewsbury Biscuits and Chocolate Almond Biscotti. And as the grand finale to the book and any of your meals, try the desserts and mithais such as Chocolate Kulfi and Chocolate and Nut Karanji. If this is making you so restless that you want to get down to riffling through the whole book right away, wait a bit, there is more sinful indulgence for breakfast! Yes, Chocolate Pancake and Chocolate Danish for you! Create some beautiful garnishes just like experts using recipes for Chocolate Arcs and Chocolate Leaves to name a couple.

Well, as this has been a chocolate-rich page, allow me to leave you to enjoy the pleasures of it. All recipes will serve four (or one or two if there is no reason to share!) and are tried and tested in my kitchen so that you have no difficulty in trying them out.

May all chocoholics pass on the good word!

Happy cooking!

Sanjeev Kapoor

Chocolate
The wonder ingredient

There are perhaps very few who do not enjoy munching on a bar of chocolate some time or the other. Eating chocolate lifts your mood, spreads a feeling of well-being! But how many of us know where this creamy, dreamy oh-so-delicious sweet something comes from? A few may be, but most of us just buy them off the shelf and pop them into our mouths whenever we feel like one. Well, here I am, with my book on chocolates that I have written especially for all you chocoholics and also for those potential chocolate lovers. This book, I promise, will give you an insight into the mysteries of this wonder ingredient. It is likely that whatever you have read about chocolate till now, you could have found it a trifle complicated, but with this book I intend to make chocolate as simple as possible for you. And I am sure after reading through these pages you will find it easy to work with this interesting ingredient, which hitherto seemed complicated!

Let us start at the very beginning. Where cooking with this ingredient is concerned, basically there are two categories of chocolate namely 'Couverture' and 'Coating' chocolate. Coating chocolate is also known as Glazing and Pate Glace. According to me it is best to use 'Couverture' chocolate and that is because it scores over its counterpart, the 'Coating' type, on a number of points, some of which are as follows:

- It provides a better flavour to the recipe
- It provides a better mouth-feel
- It makes the recipe the most appealing
- And it is healthier.

Though, the 'Coating' type can be easily handled and is cheaper than the 'Couverture' type, the above reasons are definitely important if you want to get the best results with chocolate. 'Coating' chocolate' is, most of the times, darker and bitter and is seen more in the market as it is easy to store and handle. But let that not be the reason for you to compromise on the quality. To get the best and the most premium quality of 'Couverture' chocolate, you must look for the following:

- Fruity taste
- Acidic nature
- Cocoa content
- Cocoa butter content in the chocolate.

Where does chocolate come from

Now let us get to the origins of this fantastic ingredient. I am sure all of you must be interested to know where chocolate comes from. Well, it comes from the cocoa beans of the cacao tree, which is majorly native to the tropical countries, at 15º-20° N-S of the equator on the world map.

The cocoa bean is usually divided into two components: one having the 'fats' (cocoa butter – 50-55%) and the other the 'non-fat solids', together they make cocoa mass or cocoa solids. The 'fat' or the 'cocoa butter', as it is commonly known, is colourless and is the flavour carrier which is responsible for giving the texture and mouth-feel to the chocolate. The dense and heavy 'non-fat solids' on the other hand, is the flavouring component and gives taste in the chocolate. The 'cocoa mass' when combined with sugar, vanilla and the emulsifier lecithin (usually extracted from soya) results in the dark variety of the 'Couverture' chocolate and when you combine the 'non-fat solids' with vegetable fat, sugar, vanilla and emulsifier lecithin, you have 'Coating/Glaze' chocolate.

When the 'non-fat solids' are separated from the cocoa bean, we get 'cocoa powder' with variable fat content, ranging from 8-12% to 18-24%. The quality of 'cocoa powder' is generally measured by the percentage of fat content in it – higher the percentage, the superior is the quality. 'Cocoa powder' is usually acidic in nature (pH being 5.2-6.9), so it is treated with an alkali (raising it to pH 6.0-8.8) by a process known as Dutch Process, which makes it richer, darker, less acidic and has less tendency to settle out when combined with liquids and makes it suitable for dishes that call for baking powder.

Factors affecting the quality of chocolate

Now, let us ponder over some points that play a vital role in deciding the quality of a chocolate:
On a broader aspect, I have already discussed and given you my choice of using the 'Couverture' chocolate over 'Coating' chocolate. But, technically the former variety is also better because of the amount of cocoa bean content that is present in it. The 'Couverture' chocolate is available in any range – from 50% bean quantity to 100% bean quantity. In simpler words, if a bar of 'Couverture' says 50% chocolate, it simply means that the bar has 50% cocoa beans and the rest 50% is a combination of sugar, vanilla and lecithin. The higher the percentage of cocoa beans in a 'Couverture' chocolate, the more intense is the flavour and richer is the chocolate!

Next, comes the source or origin of the cocoa bean. Some of the world's best cocoa beans come from regions such as South America, West Africa, Ecuador, Madagascar, etc.

The species of the cocoa bean is also something that would result in deciding the quality of the chocolate as a whole. The four main varieties of the cacao beans are Criollo, Forastero, Trinitario and Arriba/Nacional.

Soil quality, harvesting, fermentation process, etc. also play a major role in deciding the quality of a chocolate.

Also important are the activities that are carried out at the manufacturing site like roasting, drying, crushing, etc. which are equally important in giving a sound quality to the chocolate.

How chocolate is made

The ripe cocoa pods from the cacao tree are harvested, which further go through the following processes:

Natural Fermentation – The cocoa beans (kernels inside the pod) are covered with a white sugary pulp on the outside, which when subjected to high temperatures, ferment with the natural yeast-like components in the air, resulting in breaking and fermenting the pulp. This is an important step and takes place over five days, and during this, the taste is 'fruity' and not chocolaty.

Fermentation – This is carried out in cool places, usually for four-five days, at controlled temperatures to get 'flavour precursors.' Colour is not affected at this stage.

Drying – This process is carried out in order to reduce the moisture content that is present in the beans, and usually takes five to seven days. This is done under moderate heat in order to avoid developing of bacteria. Natural way of drying up the beans in the sun is a preferred way rather than the artificial way. The former way keeps the flavour intact unlike the artificial way, which sometimes can develop a smoky flavour.

Roasting – This is one of the most important steps in the entire process of making a chocolate. Here, the beans are roasted at temperatures ranging from 140ºC-180ºC. This way the flavour is enhanced and developed. However, the duration of roasting is determined by the size of beans and can vary from an hour to an hour-and-a-half. There are three types of roasting that take place, namely, 'whole bean roasting', 'nib roasting' and 'mass/liquor roasting.'

Breaking and Winnowing – The roasted beans are further broken down into smaller pieces and the skins are removed by a process termed as 'winnowing.' After these processes, we get what are called 'nibs.'

Crushing – This step involves reducing the broken particles further into smaller particles.

Mixing – After the beans are broken and crushed, they are transformed into the two main types called the 'dark' chocolate and the 'milk' chocolate. For dark chocolate, the crushed bean particles are mixed with sugar and for milk chocolate, the crushed bean particles are mixed with milk powder.

Refining – Particle size is further reduced to get a smooth textured chocolate.

Conching – Under controlled heat applications (45°-80°C), the melted chocolate is constantly stirred which results in the final quality and smooth texture of the chocolate. This is the step where vanilla, lecithin and extra cocoa butter are added. A normal quality of chocolate maybe conched for four to six hours whereas a supreme quality might require conching for almost 72 hours. This is where the final flavours and the aromas of a good chocolate will develop.

Tempering – Chocolate is tempered by cooling the chocolate very gradually, with agitation. At this stage the liquid or semi-liquid chocolate is turned into a solid. Large scales of tempering processes have ' temper meters' to carry out this process. An important point to remember in this process is that only the chocolate having the fat content as 'cocoa butter' needs tempering. If there are vegetable fats in it, just like there is in the 'Coating' type, then that does not require tempering. This process is what gives the chocolate its final state, shine and shortness.

Packaging and Shipping – Before packing the final product to be shipped, it is necessary to do a quality assurance. The chocolate is now shaped into coins or block forms. Once this is done, the product is finally ready to be packed. After the entire process of making of a chocolate, they are properly wrapped and sealed and made ready to be shipped to various parts of the world.

Types of chocolates

There are three basic types of chocolates:

Dark Chocolate – This type is made with a combination of the cocoa mass (cocoa butter + non-fat solids), sugar, vanilla and the emulsifier lecithin.

Milk Chocolate – This one is the result of the amalgamation of cocoa mass (cocoa butter + non-fat solids), sugar, milk powder, vanilla and the emulsifier lecithin.

White Chocolate – This type is made with only cocoa butter along with sugar, milk powder, vanilla and the emulsifier lecithin.

Apart from these, the market also has some chocolate types like 'bitter-sweet', 'semi-sweet', 'sweet-dark', etc. They are options based on the intensity of the chocolate. Do not let these terms confuse you. In case you are using any of these, make it a point to check the following so that you do not end up with poor and unsatisfactory results:
The brand, ingredients label, manufacturer's directions and finally the taste.

How to store chocolate

Now that we have travelled through the processes of making of chocolate and handling it, there is one more aspect that is left which is really important when working with this sinful ingredient – and that is – the storage. The following pointers will help you tackle the issues of storing chocolate perfectly:

In the Indian climate, ideally chocolates should be stored at temperatures ranging from 15°C to 20°C at humidity not more than 50%.

The best way to store chocolate is to put the original packing in plastic wrap, cling film or zip lock bags, place them in airtight containers and put in the refrigerator. One important point to remember is that you should never keep the chocolate in a deep freezer, as this may spoil the chocolate because of condensation that may occur.

It is also advisable to store chocolate away from strong odours as it may absorb the strong smells from other items, thus spoiling its own aroma.

Then for application of refrigerated chocolate, the best way to use it is to keep the chocolate at room temperature for about ten-fifteen minutes (to avoid temperature and humidity shock that may cause condensation and thickening) and then open the packets.

How chocolate should be melted

Here are some tips that come in handy when you go about melting the chocolate:

- Chop large chocolate blocks into smaller pieces and put in a plastic bowl. Avoid using glass or stainless steel bowls as they cause uneven heating.

- If using a Microwave oven, place the bowl in it and start the melting process from 40 seconds at 50% intensity of the Microwave. Then, take the bowl out, stir and continue this process till the complete chocolate is melted. Please do not ever keep for longer time at higher temperatures for chocolate needs delicate treatment.

- If using a double boiler, take a medium height pan filled one-fourth with water and heat it. When the water is at a simmer, reduce heat to minimum, place a bowl that fits on the mouth of the pan and start putting the chocolate in it to be melted, little at a time. One important point to remember here is that you should not boil the water as it will affect the viscosity of the chocolate and steam from boiling water may play havoc. Keep stirring the chocolate pieces till completely melted.

By now, I am sure that your interest in this wonderful ingredient has risen further than what it was before and you are now confident of trying your hand and cooking skills to dish out some amazing chocolate recipes in your kitchen. Just before I wrap up, here are some more guidelines for housewives that will help them handle this extremely delicate ingredient with utmost care:

- Remember, water is the biggest enemy of chocolate! Especially, when the chocolate is being melted for use in confectionary, candy making, tempering, etc., you should be very careful that not even a single drop of water gets into it. But if this happens by mistake, keep it aside to use in recipes where it is only an ingredient, and start afresh.

- Check for blooming and any odours in the chocolate bars. When chocolate is exposed to warm temperatures, the fat softens and chocolate is then untempered, causing light grey or white areas on the surface of the chocolate. Also, sometimes you might find small white dots on the chocolate, which is due to condensation.

- Avoid overheating of chocolate as it results in making the chocolate thick after melting.

- If there is a loss of colour in the chocolate bars, this may be due to changes in the light, temperature and humidity.

The preferred working temperatures in the Indian scenario is around 20°C with humidity not more than 50% and preferably on marble work tops. Marble helps keep the chocolate cool.

It is always good to work with clean kitchenware and work tops when handling chocolate and also advisable to keep some kitchenware separate (especially in Indian kitchens where interaction with masalas will give unwarranted flavours to your chocolate) that can be used when working with chocolate.

And this one is for all chocolate lovers – always remember to look at the ingredients printed on the packet. Chocolate with natural cocoa butter rather than vegetable fats is always more healthy. Not to forget, chocolate is good source of energy at any given time.

By now I am sure your fingers must be itching to churn out chocolate delights. If you follow the simple instructions given herein, I can assure you good results. So, go ahead and enjoy your interaction with chocolate.

Contents

Chapter 1 >

Beverages

Chocolate Lassi

{ Chocolate is mainly a western taste, while lassi is essentially Indian. This is a great way to show how the twain can meet...deliciously! }

Ingredients

1¼ cups grated dark chocolate
4 cups thick yogurt, chilled
8 tablespoons powdered sugar
A pinch of salt
4 tablespoons dark chocolate chips

Method:

1. Melt the chocolate in a double boiler. You can also melt the chocolate in a microwave-safe bowl in a microwave on HIGH for thirty seconds. Whisk well and set aside to cool down to room temperature.
2. Mix together the yogurt, sugar and salt in a bowl. Whisk until the sugar and salt are well incorporated.
3. Add the cooled melted chocolate and mix well.
4. Pour into individual glasses and serve chilled, garnished with the chocolate chips.

Eggless

Choco Frappé

{ Sometimes you need a little pick-me-up to get through a long and stressful day. And what could be better than a tall, cold glass of milky coffee spiked with the richness of chocolate! }

Ingredients

6 teaspoons instant coffee powder
8 tablespoons chocolate truffle
4 cups vanilla ice cream
2 cups milk
4 tablespoons powdered sugar
Ice cubes, as required
½ cup whipped cream
Chocolate shavings for garnishing

Method:

Eggless

1. Mix the coffee powder with three teaspoons of warm water to make a decoction.
2. Blend together four tablespoons chocolate truffle, coffee decoction, vanilla ice cream, milk, powdered sugar and ice cubes till smooth.
3. Drizzle the remaining truffle along the sides of four individual glasses to make a pattern. Pour in the coffee-chocolate mixture.
4. Put the whipped cream in a piping bag and pipe over the coffee in each glass.
5. Serve chilled, garnished with chocolate shavings.

Spiced Hot Chocolate

{ Nothing spells 'comfort' better than warm chocolate with a sparky bite. Combine the fire of spices with the heat of a hot drink and feel the magic begin! }

Method:

1. Heat the milk, cream and caster sugar together in a non-stick pan but do not let it boil.
2. Remove from the heat and transfer the hot mixture into a bowl. Add the star anise and cinnamon, cover with cling film and set aside for two to three hours.

Rocky Road Shake

{ The crunch of nuts, the gooey chew of marshmallows, the soft delight of chocolate, the cold bite of ice cream... how could heaven fit so easily in a glass! }

Ingredients

20 marshmallows
4 cups chocolate ice cream
1 cup milk
½ cup roughly chopped walnuts

Eggless

Method:

1. Chop the marshmallows.
2. Place half the marshmallows in a blender jar. Add the chocolate ice cream, milk and half the walnuts and blend well.
3. Pour into four individual glasses, garnish with the remaining walnuts and marshmallows.
4. Serve chilled.

Ingredients

2 star anise
4 one-inch cinnamon sticks
1 cup chopped dark chocolate
4 cups milk
2 cups fresh cream
¼ cup caster sugar

3. Strain the mixture into another non-stick pan and heat it again.
4. Put chopped chocolate into four individual glasses and pour the hot spiced milk into each glass. Stir well till the chocolate melts.
5. Serve hot.

Eggless

Mango Milkshake with Chocolate

{ Chocolate adds a wonderful rich flavour to almost anything it is added to. Mango is no exception. Combine the bright orange of the fruit with the dark brown of the chocolate and you have an unbeatable partnership! }

Ingredients

2 cups fresh mango pulp
4 tablespoons chocolate sauce
4 cups milk
4 tablespoons milk powder
8 tablespoons sugar
2 cups vanilla ice cream
4 tablespoons chocolate chips

Method:

1. Drizzle chocolate sauce along the sides of four individual glasses and refrigerate for fifteen to twenty minutes.
2. Blend mango pulp, milk, milk powder, sugar and vanilla ice cream till smooth. (If you are using tinned mango pulp, use only four tablespoons of sugar.)
3. Pour into the prepared glasses and serve chilled, garnished with the chocolate chips.

Eggless

yummy!

Warm Chocolate Shots

The creaminess of ice cream melted into the sweet darkness of chocolate, all spiked with the bitter wake-up call of coffee – a lovely way to make a rainy day warm and welcoming!

Ingredients

¾ cup chopped dark chocolate
½ cup milk
1 cup chocolate ice cream
2 teaspoons instant coffee powder
2 tablespoons powdered sugar

Method:

1. Place the dark chocolate in a deep microwave-safe bowl and melt in the microwave on HIGH for thirty seconds. Alternatively, melt in a double boiler. Remove and whisk well.
2. Heat the milk in a non-stick pan, but do not boil it. Add it to the chocolate and mix well. Add the chocolate ice cream and mix well.
3. Dissolve the instant coffee powder in two tablespoons of warm water and add this to chocolate-milk mixture. Add the powdered sugar and mix well.
4. Pour the mixture into eight shot glasses and serve warm.

Eggless

Chapter 2>

Breakfast

Chocolate Pancakes

Eat a good breakfast, any nutritionist will tell you. And what better way to start the day than with dainty chocolate-laden pancakes!

Ingredients

¼ cup cocoa powder
Dark chocolate chips, as required
¾ cup refined flour (maida)
1½ teaspoons baking powder
¼ teaspoon salt
1 egg
2 tablespoons caster sugar
1 cup milk
2 tablespoons melted butter + for greasing
To serve
Maple syrup, as required or
Whipped cream, as required

Method:

1. Sift the flour, baking powder, cocoa powder and salt together into a bowl.
2. Break the egg into a bowl, add caster sugar, milk and two tablespoons melted butter and whisk well.
3. Fold the flour mixture into the egg mixture and mix well till the batter is smooth and without any lumps. Chill in a refrigerator for ten to fifteen minutes.
4. Heat a non-stick tawa and grease it with a little butter. Pour a ladleful of the batter and spread it thinly. Cook, turning sides, till golden brown on both sides. Repeat the same to make the remaining pancakes.
5. Transfer onto a serving plate.
6. Serve hot drizzled with maple syrup or whipped cream.

Chef's tip: You can sprinkle some chocolate chips on one side of the pancake, fold and then serve drizzled with maple syrup.

Chocolate Waffles

{ Crispy-edged waffles are ideal to hold toppings of various kinds, from fruit to cream to, of course, chocolate sauce. Everyone will agree that a breakfast like this makes life close to perfect! }

Ingredients

½ cup chocolate sauce
¾ cup refined flour (maida)
1 teaspoon baking powder
4 eggs
4 tablespoons caster sugar
⅔ cup milk
1¼ cups fresh cream
2 tablespoons butter

Method:

1. Sift the flour and baking powder together into a bowl.
2. Break the eggs into another bowl; add the caster sugar and beat till light and fluffy. Add the milk and cream and mix well.
3. Fold the flour mixture into the egg mixture and mix well till the batter is smooth and without any lumps. Chill the batter in the refrigerator for one hour.
4. Grease a waffle-iron with a little butter and pour a ladleful of the batter on it. Close the lid. Cook for five to eight minutes or till golden brown. Repeat the procedure to make the remaining waffles.
5. Transfer the waffles onto serving plates, drizzle some chocolate sauce over them and serve hot.

Chocolate Danish Eggless

{ Bite into crisply flaky pastry and you find a pleasant surprise – a core of delightfully sinful chocolate! }

Ingredients

8 tablespoons chopped dark chocolate
2¾ cups refined flour (maida)
+ ¼ cup for layering + for dusting
1½ teaspoons salt
2 tablespoons milk powder
2 tablespoons fresh yeast
1 tablespoon sugar
1¼ cups butter
Milk, as required

Method:

1. Sift together the flour, salt and milk powder into a bowl.
2. Dissolve the yeast and sugar in two tablespoons lukewarm water in another small bowl.
3. Add the yeast mixture and one-fourth cup butter to the flour mixture. Add sufficient water and knead into a medium-hard dough. Flatten the dough slightly, wrap in cling film and chill for an hour in the refrigerator.

Nutella Toast

{ Whoever came up with the idea of making a creamy spread with hazelnuts has to be called a genius. This recipe is a great way to make a snack more than just gratifying! }

Ingredients

8 tablespoons Nutella
16 slices brown bread
24 walnut kernels, roasted and chopped

4. To make the butter layering, cream one cup butter till smooth. Add one-fourth cup flour and mix well.
5. Dust a silicon sheet with some flour or line an eight-inch rectangular tray with butter paper. Place the butter mixture on it and shape it into a rectangle. Refrigerate for an hour or till it is almost hard.
6. Remove the dough from the refrigerator and roll it into a rectangle at least three times the size of the butter rectangle.
7. Place the butter rectangle in the centre of the rolled out dough, fold over the two smaller sides first and then fold over the two longer sides and seal well to enclose the butter entirely. Ensure that the butter is not too hard while placing it on the dough. Wrap in cling film and keep it in the refrigerator for fifteen to twenty minutes.
8. Remove from the refrigerator and roll out into a half-inch thick, seven-inch by five-inch rectangle. Give it a threefold - first fold one-third of the longer side of the rectangle, then fold over the rest to overlap the first fold to make a rectangle again. Wrap in cling film and refrigerate again for half an hour.
9. Remove from the refrigerator and repeat the above process. Wrap in cling film. Refrigerate again for half an hour.
10. Remove from the refrigerator and roll out into half inch thickness. Cut into three-inch squares.
11. Place a little chopped chocolate in the centre of each square, apply a little water on the edges and join the diagonally opposite corners to make a triangle.
12. Arrange the prepared Chocolate Danish on a greased baking tray, cover with a damp piece of muslin and allow them to prove for twenty to twenty-five minutes.
13. Preheat the oven to 180°C/350°F/Gas Mark 4.
14. Uncover the tray and apply a milk wash on the triangles. Bake in the preheated oven for twenty minutes or till light golden in colour. Serve hot.

Method:

1. Cut the bread into round slices with a round cookie cutter.
2. Heat a non-stick tawa and toast the bread, turning sides, till both sides are crisp.
3. Apply Nutella evenly on all the bread slices. Sprinkle the chopped walnuts on eight slices, cover them with the remaining eight slices.
4. Serve.

Chocolate Granola Bar

{ If you have to eat health food, make sure it is delicious and has a little touch of wickedness added to it. Chocolate will do that perfectly, every time! }

Ingredients

4 tablespoons melted dark chocolate
2 cups muesli
¼ cup rice crispies
4 tablespoons honey

Method:

1. Dry-roast the muesli in a non-stick pan till crisp. Remove from the heat and cool to room temperature. Line a five-inch by seven-inch rectangular tin with cling film.
2. Combine the muesli, rice crispies, honey and melted chocolate in a bowl.
3. Transfer this mixture into the prepared tin and spread evenly. Refrigerate for forty to forty-five minutes or till set.
4. Cut into bars and serve.

Chocolate Baked Yogurt

{ Add yogurt to dessert and you feel healthier instantly. Add chocolate to anything and you feel better instantly. Combine the two – and you will be a happy person!

Ingredients

¼ cup melted dark chocolate
2 tablespoons dark chocolate chips
125 grams yogurt
100 grams condensed milk
100 grams fresh cream
Chocolate powder for dusting

Method:

1. Preheat the oven to 180°C/350°F/Gas Mark 4.
2. Pour the yogurt, condensed milk and fresh cream into a bowl and mix well together.
3. Put one-fourth of the yogurt mixture into a glass bowl, add the melted chocolate and mix well.
4. Add this mixture and chocolate chips to the remaining yogurt mixture and mix well.
5. Pour the chocolate-yogurt mixture into four individual oven-proof glasses. Place them in the preheated oven and bake for eight to ten minutes.
6. Remove from the oven and let them cool down to room temperature. Chill in the refrigerator, dust with chocolate powder and serve.

Chapter 3 >

Cakes and Pastries

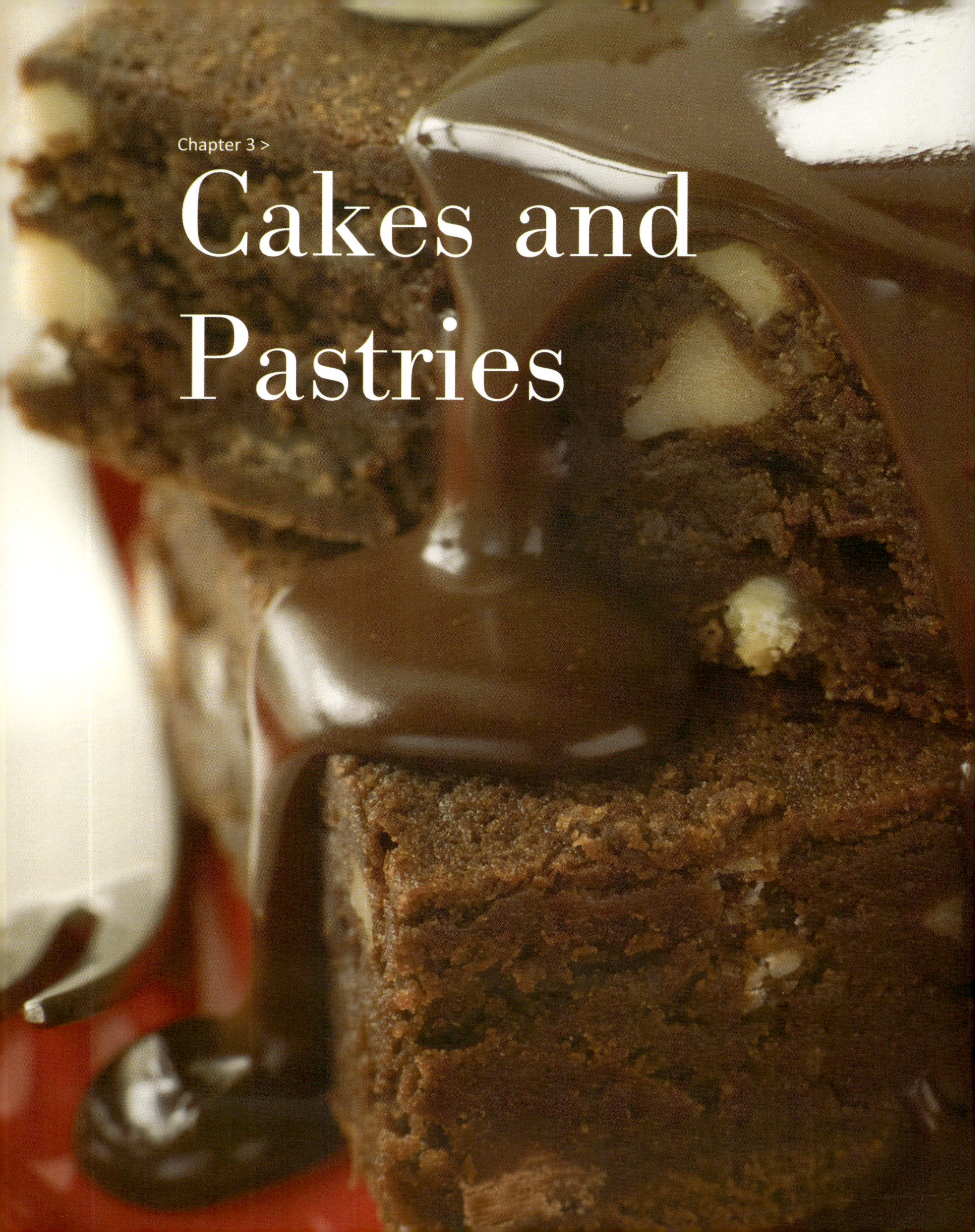

Millionaire Chocolate Brownie

{ Eat one bite of this wonderfully rich, intensely chocolatey brownie and you will feel like the most privileged person on earth! }

Ingredients

2 cups grated dark chocolate
¾ cup refined flour (maida)
A pinch of salt
¼ teaspoon soda bi-carbonate (baking soda)
¾ cup butter
¾ cup sugar
1 teaspoon vanilla essence
2 eggs
½ recipe Caramel Fudge
(See recipe Caramel and Nut Tart)
To Serve
2 scoops vanilla ice cream

Method:

1. Preheat oven to 180ºC/350°F/Gas Mark 4.
2. Sift the flour, salt and baking soda together into a bowl. Grease a six-inch square cake tin.
3. Melt the butter in a deep non-stick pan. Add the sugar and two tablespoons water and mix till sugar dissolves.
4. Remove the pan from heat, add the grated chocolate and stir till it melts. Add the vanilla essence and mix well.
5. Add one egg at a time and mix well. Add the flour mixture and mix till well incorporated.
6. Pour the batter into the greased cake tin and bake in the preheated oven for fifty-five to sixty minutes.
7. Remove from the oven and transfer to a wire rack and allow to cool slightly.
8. Halve the brownie horizontally. Spread the caramel fudge over the bottom half of the brownie and cover with the other half.
9. Cut into squares. Serve while still warm, accompanied with vanilla ice cream.

Death by Chocolate

You will not die after eating this, but you will certainly feel like you have had the ultimate experience – rich, dark, sweet, sinful... if this is death, you will come back for more!

Ingredients

Sponge Cake
2 cups refined flour (maida)
1½ teaspoons baking powder
2 cups butter
2 cups caster sugar
5 eggs
A few drops of vanilla essence
½ cup milk
⅓ cup melted dark chocolate

Sugar Syrup
¾ cup sugar

Truffle
125 grams fresh cream
250 grams dark chocolate, chopped

Chocolate Layering
1 cup chopped dark chocolate
2 tablespoons butter
¼ cup brown sugar
½ cup fresh cream
3 tablespoons coffee decoction

Method:

1. Preheat the oven to 180°C/350°F/Gas Mark 4. Grease a seven-inch round cake tin.
2. To make the sponge, sift the flour and baking powder together into a bowl. Set aside.
3. Cream together the butter and caster sugar till fluffy. Add the eggs one by one and mix till well blended. Add the vanilla essence and mix well.
4. Fold the flour into the butter mixture and mix well. Add the milk and melted chocolate and mix well.
5. Pour the batter into the greased tin and place in the preheated oven. Bake for thirty to forty minutes and remove from the oven.
6. To make the sugar syrup, heat three-fourth cup water in a deep non-stick pan. Add the sugar and stir till it dissolves completely. Remove from heat and set aside.
7. To make the truffle, heat the cream in a non-stick pan till it just begins to boil. Place the chopped chocolate in a bowl and add the cream to it. Mix well till the chocolate melts. Keep in the refrigerator to set.
8. To make the chocolate layering, melt the dark chocolate, butter and brown sugar together in a non-stick pan. Mix well till the chocolate melts.
9. Add the cream and coffee decoction and mix well. Remove from heat and allow it to cool.
10. Cut the cake into four horizontally. Drizzle the sugar syrup on each layer. Divide the chocolate layering mixture into four equal portions and spread evenly on all the four layers.
11. Place the layers one on top of the other and place the entire cake in the refrigerator for an hour.
12. Melt three-fourth of the truffle and pour on the prepared cake and pat the cake gently so that the mixture covers the cake evenly.
13. Put the remaining truffle into a piping bag and pipe out rosettes on the edges of the cake. Refrigerate the cake for half an hour.
14. Remove, cut into eight pieces and serve.

Choco Lava Cake

{ Cut into this delightful nugget and watch that stream of warm sweet chocolate ooze out, only to be captured by your spoon! }

Ingredients

125 grams plain chocolate, broken into pieces
1 tablespoon cocoa powder + for dusting
½ cup refined flour (maida) + for dusting
9 tablespoons unsalted butter + for greasing
4 eggs
6 tablespoons powdered sugar
½ teaspoon baking powder

Method:

1. Preheat the oven to 180°C/350°F/Gas Mark 4. Grease the muffin moulds, dust with flour and remove excess flour.
2. Put the chocolate in a microwave-safe bowl, add the butter and melt in the microwave oven on HIGH for one minute. Remove the bowl from oven and stir the contents briskly.
3. Break the eggs into another bowl. Add powdered sugar and blend with a hand blender till light and frothy. Sift the cocoa powder directly in the mixture and mix.
4. Add the melted chocolate-butter mixture and mix.
5. Sift the flour and baking powder directly into the bowl and blend with the hand blender till smooth.
6. Pour the batter into the muffin moulds, taking care not to fill up to the top.
7. Place the moulds in the preheated oven and bake for seven to eight minutes.
8. Take the moulds out of the oven, loosen the edges carefully with a knife. Carefully remove cakes from moulds directly onto a serving plate and serve hot.

Eggless Black Forest Gâteau

Exquisite is the word for this! In looks and taste, here is a cake that doubles up as a birthday cake many times over!

Ingredients

50 grams cocoa powder
Chocolate curls or grated chocolate, as required
110 grams refined flour (maida)
½ teaspoon baking powder
½ teaspoon soda bi-carbonate (baking soda)
120 grams butter
200 grams condensed milk
1 teaspoon vanilla essence
5 tablespoons milk
½ cup tinned cherries, with syrup
2 cups whipping cream

Method:

1. Preheat the oven to 180°C/350°F/Gas Mark 4. Grease a five-and-a-half-inch round cake tin.
2. Sift the flour, cocoa powder, baking powder and baking soda together into a bowl.
3. Cream the butter and condensed milk together in another bowl till fluffy. Add the vanilla essence and mix well.
4. Fold the flour into the butter mixture gently, adding the milk as you mix. Transfer the mixture into the greased cake tin and bake for twenty to twenty-five minutes.
5. Remove the cake from the oven and leave the cake in the tin for five minutes to cool slightly. Turn out onto a wire rack, and leave to cool.
6. Cut the cake into half horizontally and sprinkle each half with cherry syrup from the tinned cherries.
7. Whip the cream until stiff. Place the bottom half of the cake on a serving plate and spread half the whipped cream over it. Cover with the top half of the cake. Spread the remaining cream over the top and sides.
8. Decorate the gâteau with chocolate curls or grated chocolate and cherries and chill in the refrigerator.
9. Cut into wedges and serve chilled.

Devil's Food Cake

{ Your wicked side will emerge when you take your first bite of this devilish 'n dense chocolate cake. Go on, we dare you! }

Ingredients

1½ cups refined flour (maida)
1 teaspoon baking powder
½ teaspoon salt
1 teaspoon soda bi-carbonate (baking soda)
60 grams butter
1 cup powdered sugar
2 eggs
60 grams cooking chocolate
½ cup milk
½ teaspoon lemon juice
1 teaspoon vanilla essence

Method:

1. Preheat the oven to 180°C/350°F/Gas Mark 4. Grease a nine-inch round cake tin.
2. Sift the flour, baking powder, salt and baking soda together in a bowl.
3. Cream the butter and sugar in another bowl until light and fluffy. Add the eggs one at a time and beat well after each addition.
4. Melt the chocolate in half a cup of boiling water. Cool slightly. Stir this into the egg mixture.
5. Fold in the flour mixture, milk, lemon juice and vanilla essence, mixing gently till well blended.
6. Pour into the greased tin and bake in the preheated oven for about twenty-five minutes. Remove from the oven, place the tin on a wire rack and allow cake to cool completely in the tin.
7. Remove from mould, slice and serve.

Pressure Cooker Eggless Chocolate Cake

{ Let us not bake a cake today...but cook it in the pressure cooker! A novel idea, an excellent recipe and a superb cake to offer! }

Ingredients

100 grams dark cooking chocolate
1 cup butter
1 1/3 cups refined flour (maida)
2 teaspoons baking powder
1 cup + 2 tablespoons powdered sugar
1 teaspoon vanilla essence
¾ cup milk
½ cup walnuts kernels
Butter for greasing

Method:

1. Remove the whistle of the pressure cooker. Add two cups water. Place a stainless steel stand in such a way that the cake tin does not come in direct contact with the water.
2. Grate the chocolate. Cut the butter into cubes. Melt butter and chocolate in a Microwave-safe bowl in the Microwave oven on HIGH for one minute.
3. In another bowl sift flour and baking powder.
4. Mix the melted butter and chocolate well. Add powdered sugar, vanilla essence and mix. Add the flour mixture and mix. Correct the consistency by adding milk. Add walnuts and mix gently.
5. Transfer the mixture into a small non-stick square cake tin. Place the cake tin on the stainless steel stand kept inside the cooker. Put lid on the cooker and place it on heat and cook for seventy-five to ninety minutes or till done. To check, insert a skewer in the cake and if it comes out clean, the cake is done. Remove tin from cooker and let it stand for five minutes.
6. Remove cake from the tin and cool on a wire rack. Slice and serve.

Opera Cake

{ It may sound complicated, but working through this recipe will be well worth the trouble once you hear the rave reviews you get! }

Ingredients

210 grams refined flour (maida)
¾ teaspoon baking powder
¾ teaspoon soda bi-carbonate (baking soda)
180 grams butter
300 grams condensed milk
1 teaspoon vanilla essence
112 ml milk

Butter Cream
1½ cups chopped dark chocolate
500 grams butter
500 grams icing sugar
2 tablespoons coffee powder
4 tablespoons Nutella
¾ cup fresh cream

Sugar Syrup
1 cup sugar

Method:

1. Preheat the oven to 180°C/350°F/Gas Mark 4. Grease a five-and-a-half-inch round cake tin.
2. Sift the flour, baking powder and baking soda together into a bowl.
3. Cream the butter and condensed milk together in another bowl till fluffy. Add the vanilla essence and mix well. Fold in the flour into the butter mixture gently, adding the milk as you mix. Transfer the batter into the greased cake tin and bake for twenty to twenty-five minutes. Remove the cake from the oven and leave the cake in the tin for five minutes to cool slightly. Turn out onto a wire rack, and leave to cool.
4. To make the butter cream, cream the butter and icing sugar together in a bowl till light and fluffy. Divide the mixture into three equal parts to make three different flavoured butter creams.
5. To make coffee-butter cream, heat one-fourth cup water and add coffee powder and mix well. Take one portion of the butter cream and add the coffee decoction to it. Mix well and set aside.
6. To make the hazelnut-butter cream, take the second portion of the butter cream and add Nutella to it. Mix well and set aside.
7. To make the chocolate-butter cream, heat the fresh cream in a non-stick pan. Add the chopped chocolate to it and mix well till the chocolate melts. Divide this mixture into two and add the third portion of the butter cream to one portion of the choco-cream mixture.
8. To make sugar syrup, boil one cup water in a deep non-stick pan. Add sugar to it and stir till it dissolves completely. Remove from heat and set aside.

9. Cut the cake horizontally into seven equal layers.
10. Place one layer on a worktop and drizzle with some sugar syrup. Spread half the coffee-butter cream evenly on it.
11. Place the second layer on top of the first layer and drizzle with some sugar syrup. Spread half the hazelnut-butter cream evenly on it.
12. Place the third layer on top of the second layer and drizzle with some sugar syrup. Spread half the chocolate-butter cream evenly on it.
13. Repeat the above procedure for the fourth, fifth and sixth layers. Place the seventh layer on the top and keep in the refrigerator for an hour.
14. Remove the layered cake from the refrigerator and trim the edges to give it a good finish. Pour the remaining choco-cream mixture on top and decorate as you wish.
15. Cut into wedges or pieces and serve.

Chocolate Swiss Roll

{ The traditional Swiss roll uses cream and jam. This one takes a different route, with various kinds of chocolate added to make life more interesting! }

Ingredients

1½ cups chopped dark chocolate
¼ cup cocoa powder
¼ cup white chocolate chips
¼ cup + 2 tablespoons caster sugar
3 eggs
A few drops of vanilla essence
½ cup refined flour (maida)
½ cup fresh cream
½ cup butter + for greasing
½ cup icing sugar
½ cup sugar syrup

Method:

1. Preheat the oven to 220°C/425°F/Gas Mark 7. Grease an eight-inch rectangular cake tin.
2. Whisk together the caster sugar and eggs in a bowl till light and creamy. Add the vanilla essence and mix well.
3. Sift the flour and cocoa powder and fold in the egg mixture. Pour the mixture into the greased tin and spread evenly. Place in the preheated oven and bake for ten to twelve minutes.
4. To make the chocolate ganache, heat the cream in a non-stick pan. Once it comes to a boil, take the pan off the heat and add one cup dark chocolate. Mix well and set aside.
5. To make the chocolate-butter-cream icing, melt half cup dark chocolate in a microwave on HIGH for one minute. Allow to cool down to room temperature.
6. Cream the butter and icing sugar in another bowl till light and creamy. Add a small portion of the mixture to the melted chocolate and mix well. Now add the chocolate mixture to the butter-cream icing and mix well.
7. Unmould the cake from the tin and drizzle with the sugar syrup.
8. Spread the chocolate-butter-cream icing evenly on the cake.
9. Sprinkle the white chocolate chips on the butter-cream icing layer and roll up the sponge.
10. Place the prepared Swiss roll on a wire rack and drizzle the chocolate ganache.
11. Refrigerate for fifteen to twenty minutes. Cut into slices and serve.

Gooey Chocolate Cake

{ If it is cake, it is best
that it is chocolate cake.
And if it is gooey,
it will be even better.
Try this and you will
never go back to
any other kind of cake!

Ingredients

2 cups chopped dark chocolate
½ cup + ⅓ cup butter
5 eggs, separated
¼ cup + 2 tablespoons sugar
¾ cup refined flour (maida)
A pinch of salt

Method:

1. Preheat oven to 180°C/350°F/Gas Mark 4.
2. Place the chocolate and butter in a microwave-safe bowl and melt on HIGH for one minute. Allow to cool.
3. Place the egg yolks and sugar in a bowl. Whisk till thick and creamy. Add the melted chocolate-butter mixture and mix well.
4. Sift the flour directly into the mixture and fold it in slowly.
5. Whisk the egg whites with salt until they form soft peaks and fold into the batter.
6. Pour the batter into paper cups and place in the preheated oven. Bake for ten minutes or until firm to touch.
7. Remove from the oven and allow to cool. Serve.

Chocolate Rum Balls

{ A new high, a truly enticing way to get there – add the wicked sting of rum to the sweet darkness of chocolate and watch life get lighter, brighter and a whole lot more fun! }

Eggless

Ingredients

2 cups crumbled chocolate sponge cake
2 tablespoons rum
½ cup crushed walnut kernels
½ cup crushed almonds
½ cup chocolate sauce
Coating
50 grams chopped dark chocolate
1 tablespoon cream

Method:

1. Mix together the crumbled cake, walnuts, almonds, chocolate sauce and rum to make a soft dough.
2. Divide into ten equal portions and shape them into balls. Place them in the refrigerator.
3. To make the coating, melt the chocolate in a double boiler. Add the cream and mix well. Set aside to cool.
4. Coat the rum balls with this mixture and chill them again before serving.

Chocolate Mawa Cupcake

{ The well-known mawa cake gets a new avatar with chocolate added. Isn't that all about making a good thing even better? }

Ingredients

½ cup chocolate chips
200 grams mawa/khoya, crumbled
140 grams refined flour (maida)
½ teaspoon baking powder
½ teaspoon soda bi-carbonate (baking soda)
120 grams butter
250 grams (1 cup) condensed milk
1 teaspoon vanilla essence
80 millilitres milk

Method:

1. Preheat the oven to 180°C/350°F/Gas Mark 4.
2. Sift the flour with baking powder and baking soda into a deep bowl.
3. In another bowl, cream the butter and condensed milk together till light and fluffy. Add the vanilla essence and mix well.
4. Fold the flour lightly into the butter mixture. Add the milk and mawa and mix well.
5. Arrange the cupcake moulds on a baking tray and pour the batter evenly into each mould. Do not fill them up to the top.
6. Sprinkle chocolate chips on top and place the tray in the preheated oven. Bake for twenty to twenty-five minutes.
7. Remove from moulds and serve.

Caramel and Nut Tart

{ Chewy, crunchy, soft, sweet – this one combines all of these to make a delicious and fabulous dessert! }

Ingredients

Caramel Fudge
400 grams condensed milk
Decoration
1 cup crushed mixed fruit nougat
Pastry Crust
¾ cup icing sugar
1 cup butter
¾ egg
1¼ cups refined flour (maida), sifted
A few drops of vanilla essence
Chocolate Truffle
⅓ cup fresh cream
⅔ cup chopped milk chocolate

Method:

1. To make the pastry crust, cream the icing sugar and butter together till fluffy.
2. Add the egg and mix again. Add the flour and mix well. Add the vanilla essence and mix again.
3. Place the mixture in the refrigerator for half an hour or till firm.
4. Roll out the pastry crust into half-inch thickness and line an eight-inch round tart mould with it evenly. Place in the refrigerator for another half an hour.
5. Preheat the oven to 180°C/350°F/Gas Mark 4.
6. Remove the tart mould from the refrigerator and trim the excess pastry with the help of a sharp knife. Pierce the centre with a fork and bake the crust bind in the preheated oven for twenty to twenty-five minutes or till light golden in colour.
7. Remove from the oven and allow to cool down to room temperature.
8. To make the caramel, boil four cups of water in a deep non-stick pan and place the condensed milk tin in it. Simmer for one to one and a half hours. Add more water as necessary to ensure that the tin is submerged in hot water.
9. Remove and cool completely. Open the tin and transfer the condensed milk into a bowl. Set aside.
10. To make the chocolate truffle, heat cream in a non-stick pan till it just reaches the boiling point. Place the chopped chocolate in a bowl and add the hot cream; mix till well blended.
11. Spread half the caramel evenly on the base of the tart. Spread the chocolate truffle on this layer and refrigerate for half an hour or till properly set.
12. Sprinkle crushed nougat on top and cut into eight pieces. Serve.

Note: Extra caramel fudge can be used in Caramel Centered Chocolates.

Chocolate Pie

{ Who would have thought that chocolate in a pie would be such a happy experience? Try it, you will know! }

Ingredients

½ cup white chocolate chips

Pastry Crust

¾ cup icing sugar

1 cup butter

¾ egg

1½ cups refined flour (maida)

A few drops of vanilla essence

Chocolate Ganache

1 cup fresh cream

1 cup chopped milk chocolate

Chocolate Truffle

¼ cup + 2 tablespoons fresh cream

¾ cup chopped milk chocolate

Method:

1. To make the pastry crust, cream the icing sugar and butter together till fluffy.
2. Add the egg and mix again. Add the flour and mix well. Add the vanilla essence and mix again.
3. Place the mixture in the refrigerator for half an hour or till firm.
4. Roll out the pastry into half-inch thickness and line an eight-inch round tart mould evenly. Place in the refrigerator for another half an hour.
5. Preheat the oven to 180°C/350°F/Gas Mark 4.
6. Remove the tart mould from the refrigerator and cut off the excess paste with the help of a knife. Pierce the centre with a fork and bake in the preheated oven for twenty to twenty-five minutes or till light golden in colour.
7. Remove from oven and allow it to cool down to room temperature.
8. To make the chocolate ganache, heat the cream in a non-stick pan till it just begins to boil. Place the milk chocolate in a bowl and add the hot cream to it. Mix well.
9. Pour the chocolate ganache into the baked pastry and spread evenly. Refrigerate for half an hour or till properly set.
10. To make the chocolate truffle, heat the cream in another non-stick pan till it just begins to boil. Place the chopped chocolate in a bowl and add the hot cream to it. Mix well.
11. Pour it over the ganache layer and refrigerate for half an hour or till properly set.
12. Sprinkle chocolate chips on top and cut into eight pieces. Serve.

Note: If you make the truffle in advance and it sets by the time it is needed, melt it slightly over low heat

Eggless Brownie

This recipe has no eggs, but the brownies come out light, sweet and absolutely luscious. Go on, try it!

Ingredients

100 grams dark chocolate, grated
1⅓ cups refined flour (maida)
2 teaspoons baking powder
130 grams butter
1 cup + 1½ tablespoons caster sugar
1 teaspoon vanilla essence
½ cup chopped walnuts
½ cup milk

Method:

1. Preheat oven to 180°C/350°F/Gas Mark 4. Grease an eight-inch square cake tin.
2. Sift the flour and baking powder together into a bowl.
3. Combine together the chocolate and butter in a large microwave bowl and soften, uncovered, for a minute in the microwave oven on HIGH. Alternatively, melt it in a double boiler.
4. Beat in the sugar and vanilla essence and blend well. Add the flour mixture, chopped walnuts and milk and mix well.
5. Pour the mixture into the greased cake tin.
6. Bake in the preheated oven for twenty-five to thirty minutes. Remove from the oven and transfer to a wire rack to cool. Cut into squares and serve.

Note: A double boiler is easily installed. Take a small vessel and pour some water in it. Allow it to come to a boil. Place the ingredients that need to be cooked or melted in another vessel that is larger in size. Place the larger vessel on the smaller one and allow the steam from the boiling water to cook/melt the ingredients.

Chocolate and Coconut Soft Cake

{ Coconut and chocolate make for an unexpectedly yummy combination. This one will make you wonder why you never tried putting the two together – they add up to a divine dessert! }

Ingredients

150 grams dark chocolate, melted
80 grams desiccated coconut
250 grams butter
180 grams icing sugar
80 grams refined flour (maida)
7 eggs
80 grams caster sugar

Method:

1. Preheat the oven to 180°C/350°F/Gas Mark 4. Grease a seven-and-a-half-inch round cake tin.
2. Cream the butter and icing sugar together in a bowl with an electric blender till light.
3. Sift the flour directly into the butter-sugar mixture and fold it in.
4. In another bowl, beat the eggs and caster sugar together until fluffy. Fold this lightly into the above mixture.
5. Add the desiccated coconut and melted dark chocolate and mix lightly.
6. Pour the batter into the greased cake tin and place in the preheated oven. Bake for twenty to twenty-five minutes.
7. Remove from mould and cool. Cut into pieces and serve.

Chapter 4 >

Mousse and Cheesecakes

NINE OUT OF TEN DOCTORS LIKE

CHOCOLATE

THE TENTH SIMPLY LOVES IT

Chocolate Mille Feuille

Anything that has chocolate in it can be eaten over and over again. And when that chocolate comes in layers of hard and soft, the pleasure goes on and on...

Ingredients

Chocolate Mousse
½ cup chopped dark chocolate
1½ egg yolks
1¼ teaspoons caster sugar
3 tablespoons milk
⅓ cup fresh cream

Chocolate Planks
125 grams chopped dark chocolate

Method:

1. To make the chocolate mousse, cook the egg yolks and caster sugar in a double boiler, stirring, till thick or till it coats the back of the ladle. Remove from the heat.

continued... →

Chocolate and Almond Mousse

The smoothness of mousse works wonderfully with the crunch of nuts in this mélange of chocolate and almonds. The perfect dessert!

Ingredients

1 cup chopped dark chocolate
1 cup + 2 tablespoons blanched and chopped almonds
3 egg yolks
2½ teaspoons caster sugar
⅓ cup milk
¾ cup fresh cream

Method:

1. Cook the egg yolks and caster sugar in a double boiler, stirring, till thick or till it coats the back of the ladle. Remove from the heat.
2. Heat the milk in a non-stick pan, but do not boil. Add the milk to the egg mixture and mix well.
3. Place the chopped chocolate in a deep bowl and pour the milk-egg mixture over it and mix till the chocolate melts.
4. Beat the fresh cream lightly and fold into the chocolate mixture.
5. Add one cup almonds and mix well. Place the bowl in the refrigerator for ten to fifteen minutes or till it thickens.
6. Put the mixture into a piping bag and pipe the mousse into four shot glasses. Sprinkle the remaining almonds on top and refrigerate for half an hour.
7. Serve chilled.

---

2. Heat the milk in a non-stick pan but do not boil it. Add this to the egg mixture and mix well.
3. Place the chocolate in a bowl and pour the milk-egg mixture over it and mix till the chocolate melts.
4. Beat the fresh cream lightly and fold into the chocolate mixture. Refrigerate the mixture for one hour.
5. To make the chocolate planks, melt the dark chocolate in a microwave-safe bowl and melt on microwave HIGH for about thirty seconds. Remove from the heat and stir continuously till it cools down to room temperature.
6. Spread the mixture uniformly on a silicon sheet. Once the chocolate is semi-set, cut three-inch by one-inch planks using a measuring scale. Place the silicon sheet in the refrigerator for ten to fifteen minutes so that the chocolate is completely set.
7. Transfer the set planks onto a plate.
8. Arrange four of them on a serving plate and pipe a little of the chocolate mousse on them. Cover each plank with another plank. Repeat this procedure until all the planks are used.
9. Pipe rosettes with the remaining mousse on the uppermost planks. Place in the freezer for fifteen to twenty minutes.
10. Serve chilled.

Brownie Cheesecake

{ Add the delicious sweetness of chocolate brownies to the tangy smoothness of cheeseand yogurt and you could be on your way to a wonderful new world of taste and texture! }

Ingredients

100 grams dark chocolate
1 cup refined flour (maida)
1 teaspoon baking powder
90 grams butter + for greasing
¾ cup caster sugar
2 eggs
1 teaspoon vanilla essence
½ cup chopped walnuts

Filling
1 tablespoon gelatine
225 grams unsalted cheese spread
⅔ cup yogurt
7 tablespoons sugar
1 teaspoon vanilla essence
2 egg whites

Method:

1. Preheat the oven to 180°C/350°F/Gas Mark 4. Grease individual spring form cake tins.
2. Sift the flour and baking powder together into a bcwl.
3. Combine the chocolate and butter in a large microwave-safe bowl and soften, uncovered, for a minute in a microwave on HIGH or alternatively melt it in a double boiler.
4. Beat in the sugar, eggs and vanilla essence and blend well. Add the sifted flour and walnuts and mix well.
5. Transfer the batter into the prepared cake tins and bake in the preheated oven for forty-five minutes.
6. Remove from the oven and allow the brownies to cool in the tins.
7. To make the filling, take the gelatine in a bowl and add five tablespoons water and set aside for two to three minutes. Stand the bowl over a pan of simmering water and stir until the gelatine is completely dissolved. Set aside to cool slightly.
8. Beat the cheese spread, yogurt, sugar and vanilla essence together in another bowl till well blended. Add the dissolved gelatine and mix.
9. Whisk the egg whites in a clean bowl till stiff. Fold it into the cheese mixture and spoon it over the brownie bases in the tins and level the surface. Chill in a refrigerator for at least four hours or until set.
10. Release the cheesecake carefully from the spring form tin and transfer onto a serving plate.
11. Serve with toppings of your choice.

Chocoholic

There can be nothing better than the creamy deliciousness of chocolate. But when it comes in three different intensities, the world just seems to be such a delightful place!

Ingredients

¾ cup melted milk chocolate
¾ cup melted white chocolate
¾ cup melted dark chocolate
1½ cups fresh cream
1½ cups whipped cream
4 teaspoons chocolate powder, or
4 teaspoons white chocolate chips

Method:

1. Heat the fresh cream in a non-stick pan. When it is about to come to a boil, remove the pan from heat.
2. In a glass bowl, add the milk chocolate and half cup of hot fresh cream. Whisk well and set aside to cool. Once cooled, fold in half cup of whipped cream and mix well. Set aside.
3. Repeat this same procedure using the melted white chocolate and melted dark chocolate as well.
4. Pour the three types of prepared mousse into three different piping bags.
5. Take four individual shot glasses and fill one-third of each glass with the milk chocolate mousse. Refrigerate for fifteen minutes or till set.
6. Remove from the refrigerator and top it up with the white chocolate mousse so that each shot glass is about two-third full. Refrigerate for fifteen minutes or till set.
7. Remove from the refrigerator and fill up all the shot glasses with dark chocolate mousse. Sprinkle each with chocolate powder.
8. Refrigerate for half an hour at least and serve chilled.

Note: You can serve this decorated with white chocolate chips.

Chapter 5 >

Chocolate Making

Caramel Centered Chocolates

{ Crack open the shell of this sweet morsel and find luscious soft and sweet caramel. A perfect accompaniment for that rom-com on TV! }

Ingredients

1 cup chopped milk chocolate

1 cup condensed milk

Method:

1. Wipe the chocolate moulds clean and dry with a tissue paper.
2. Melt the chocolate in a double boiler. Remove from the heat and stir it well to temper the chocolate till the temperature falls to 30°C.
3. Pour the melted chocolate into the moulds, covering the sides evenly.
4. Turn the moulds upside down over a bowl and scrape off the excess dripping chocolate. Rest on a cooling rack till set.
5. Heat the condensed milk in a non-stick pan. Cook till the mixture turns light brown in colour. As it starts thickening, take the pan off the heat and set aside to cool.
6. Pour the cooked condensed milk into piping bags and pipe into the prepared chocolate shells. Do not fill them completely.
7. Melt the remaining chocolate again in a microwave. Remove from the oven and stir well to temper the chocolate till the temperature falls to 30°C.
8. Pour the melted chocolate on top of the filled shells and with the help of a scraper spread a thin layer on top of the mould and scrape off the excess chocolate.
9. Refrigerate the moulds for ten to fifteen minutes or till the chocolate sets.
10. Remove from moulds and serve.

Eggless

Chocolate Rocks

Chocolate does indeed rock when you add the nutty crunch of almonds, pistachios and cashews!

Ingredients

250 grams dark chocolate, grated
½ cup almonds, chopped
¼ cup cashew nuts, chopped
¼ cup pistachios, chopped
¼ cup raisins

Method:

1. Dry-roast the almonds, cashew nuts and pistachios in a non-stick pan on low heat till lightly browned. Remove from the heat and add the raisins and mix well.
2. Melt the chocolate in a double boiler. Whisk till smooth.
3. Add the roasted dried fruit to the melted chocolate in batches. Mix well.
4. Place a spoonful of the choco-nut mixture on a silicon sheet and shape into a ball. You can also use a butter paper instead of silicon sheet. Roll the rest of the chocolate mixture in the same way.
5. Place the silicon sheet on a tray and keep it in the refrigerator for fifteen to twenty minutes.
6. Serve immediately.
7. You can wrap the balls up and use the candy as gifts.

Moulded Chocolate

{ Who doesn't like biting into a candy and finding a little surprise hidden inside? And if it is a contrast to the chocolate shell, even better! }

Ingredients

1 cup chopped dark chocolate
1 cup chopped milk chocolate
Filling
1 cup fresh cream
2 teaspoons caster sugar
1 tablespoon strawberry crush
¾ tablespoon instant coffee powder

Eggless

Method:

1. Wipe the chocolate moulds clean and dry with a tissue paper.
2. To make dark chocolate shells, melt the dark chocolate in a double boiler. Remove from the heat and stir well to temper the chocolate till the temperature falls to 32°C.
3. Pour the melted chocolate into the moulds, covering the sides evenly. Turn the moulds upside down over a bowl and scrape the dripping excess chocolate. Rest on a cooling rack till set.
4. To make milk chocolate shells, melt the milk chocolate in a double boiler. Remove from heat and stir well to temper the chocolate till the temperature falls to 30°C.
5. Pour the melted chocolate into the moulds, covering the sides evenly. Turn the moulds upside down over a bowl and scrape the dripping excess chocolate. Rest on a cooling rack till set.
6. To make the filling, heat the cream in a non-stick pan. Add the caster sugar and stir till the sugar melts. Take the pan off the heat and divide the mixture equally into two bowls.
7. Add the strawberry crush to one bowl and coffee powder to the other. Mix well.
8. Pour the strawberry filling into the dark chocolate shells. Do not fill them completely.
9. Melt the remaining dark chocolate again in a microwave. Remove from the oven and stir well - i.e: temper the chocolate till the temperature falls to 32°C.
10. Pour the melted chocolate over the filled shells and with the help of a scraper spread a thin layer on top of the mould and scrape off the excess chocolate.
11. Refrigerate the moulds for ten to fifteen minutes or till the chocolate sets.
12. Pour the coffee filling into the milk chocolate shells. Do not fill them completely.
13. Melt the remaining milk chocolate again in a microwave. Remove from the oven and stir well - i.e: temper the chocolate till the temperature falls to 30°C.
14. Pour the melted chocolate on top of the filled shells and with the help of a scraper spread a thin layer on top of the mould and scrape off the excess chocolate.
15. Refrigerate the moulds for ten to fifteen minutes or till the chocolate sets.
16. Remove from mould and serve.

Chocolate Shells { The perfect base for all you can create! }

Ingredients

1 cup chopped dark chocolate

Method:

1. Wipe the chocolate moulds clean and dry with tissue paper.
2. Melt the chocolate in a double boiler. Remove from heat and stir well to temper the chocolate till the temperature falls to 30°C.
3. Pour the melted chocolate into the moulds, covering the sides evenly.
4. Turn the moulds upside down over a bowl and scrape off the dripping excess chocolate. Rest the moulds on a cooling rack till set.
5. Use as required.

Pralines

Bite into the luscious darkness of chocolate and find a sweet, crunchy core – delicious!

Ingredients

2 cups chopped dark chocolate
Nougat
½ cup sugar
½ cup chopped nuts (cashew nuts, almonds)

Method:

1. To make nougat, caramelise the sugar in a non-stick pan till light brown. Add the chopped nuts and mix well till the caramel coats them evenly.
2. Remove the mixture from the heat and spread evenly on a silicon mat. Allow it to cool. When cooled, crush it lightly.
3. Wipe the chocolate moulds clean and dry with a tissue paper.
4. Melt the chocolate in a double boiler. Remove from heat and stir well to temper the chocolate till the temperature falls to 32°C.
5. Pour a little melted chocolate into the moulds, covering the sides evenly.
6. Holding the moulds upside down over a bowl, scrape off dripping excess chocolate. Rest upright on a cooling rack till set.
7. Place one teaspoon of crushed nougat into each shell.
8. Melt the remaining chocolate again in a microwave and stir till the temperature falls to 32°C. Pour the melted chocolate on top of the nougat and spread it evenly with a scraper. Scrape off the excess chocolate. Rest upright on a cooling rack till set.
9. Remove from moulds and serve.

Eggless

Rice Crispy Bar

{ There's nothing like a gentle snap, crackle and pop to make chocolate more interesting than it already is. And rice crispies do that so well! }

Ingredients

2 cups puffed rice (murmura)
2 tablespoons butter + for greasing
½ cup grated dark chocolate
1 tablespoon peanut butter
½ cup roasted and crushed peanuts
½ cup grated white chocolate

Method:

1. Heat one tablespoon butter in a non-stick pan. Add the dark chocolate and once it melts, add one cup puffed rice, half tablespoon peanut butter and half the crushed peanuts. Mix well. Grease a five-inch by seven-inch aluminum tray with butter. Spread the mixture evenly into the tray and set aside.
2. Repeat the above procedure with white chocolate and remaining ingredients.
3. Spread this evenly on top of the dark chocolate layer.
4. Allow to cool to room temperature and refrigerate for fifteen to twenty minutes.
5. Cut into desired shapes and serve.

Eggless

Chocolate Paan

{ A meal in India will traditionally end with a paan. This is an unconventional way of eating the betel leaf-wrapped digestive....but certainly a delicious one! }

Ingredients

1 cup chopped milk chocolate
2 ready made meetha paan

Method:

1. Wipe the chocolate moulds clean and dry with a tissue paper..
2. Place the chocolate in a microwave-safe bowl and melt in a microwave on HIGH for one minute. Remove the bowl from the microwave and whisk well till the temperature comes down to 30 °C.
3. Pour the melted chocolate in the moulds and rotate them so that the sides of the moulds are coated evenly.
4. Turn the moulds upside down over the bowl to drip off the excess chocolate. Rest the moulds on a cooling rack till set.
5. Coarsely blend the paan in the blender. Divide the paan mixture into as many equal portions as the number of moulds and stuff the mixture into the prepared chocolate shells.
6. Melt the remaining chocolate again in the microwave on HIGH for one minute. Remove from the microwave and whisk well till the temperature comes down to 30 °C.
7. Pour the melted chocolate on top of the paan stuffing. Scrape off any excess chocolate.
8. Refrigerate the moulds for ten to fifteen minutes or till the chocolate sets.
9. Remove from moulds and serve..

Eggless

Wafer Chocolate

{ Remember when you were a child and your mother put a chocolate wafer into your lunch dabba? Now you can put them in your box yourself! }

Ingredients

1 cup chopped dark chocolate
¼ cup chopped white chocolate
8 wafer biscuits
1 cup condensed milk
4 tablespoons crushed butterscotch pearls

Method:

1. Cook the condensed milk in a non-stick pan on low heat, stirring continuously, till it develops a toffee-like texture and is reduced to half its original volume. Take the pan off the heat and set aside.
2. Arrange four wafer biscuits on a large plate and apply the reduced condensed milk on one side of each wafer biscuit.
3. Sprinkle one tablespoon crushed butterscotch pearls on each of these four wafer biscuits. Drizzle a little of the reduced condensed milk. Cover with the remaining four wafer biscuits to make sandwiches. Press very lightly.
4. Melt the dark chocolate in a microwave-safe bowl in a microwave oven on HIGH for one minute and let it cool.
5. Dip the wafer biscuit sandwiches in the melted dark chocolate and coat them evenly, turning them with a fork. Place on a wire rack.
6. Tap the sandwiches lightly so that the excess chocolate drips down. Refrigerate for ten to fifteen minutes or till set.
7. Melt the white chocolate in a microwave-safe bowl in a microwave oven on HIGH for thirty seconds. Cool and pour into a small piping bag with pointed nozzle. Drizzle over the prepared chocolates in a pattern.
8. Serve when set.

Eggless

Chapter 6 >

Tea Time Snacks

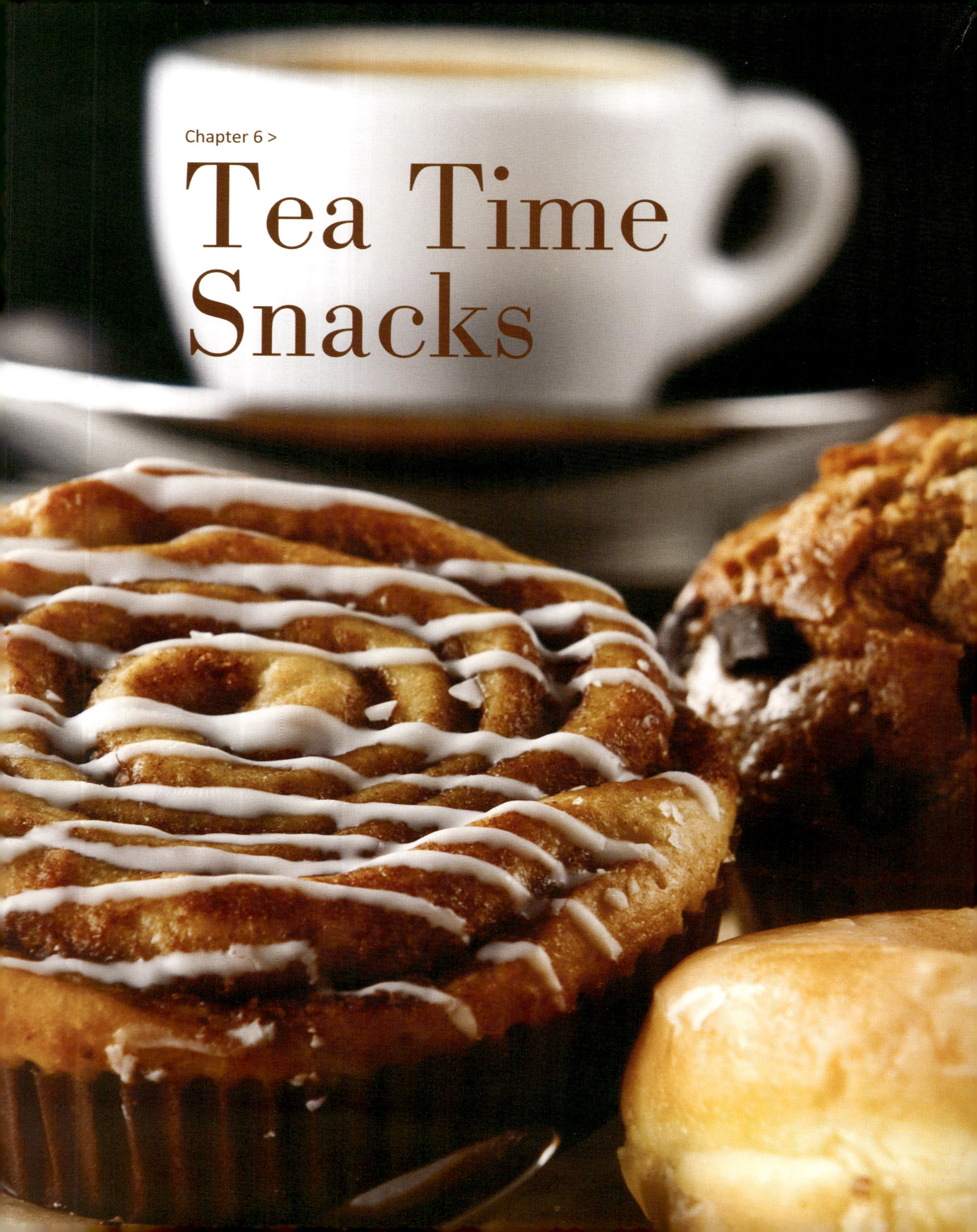

Chocolate Chip Cookies

{ Totally chocolate! There is some comfort in this madness.... }

Ingredients

1 cup dark chocolate chips
2 cups refined flour (maida)
¾ cup butter
¾ cup caster sugar
½ cup brown sugar
1 egg
A few drops of vanilla essence

Method:

1. Sift the flour into a bowl. Add the chocolate chips and mix well. Set aside.
2. Place the butter with caster sugar and brown sugar in a bowl and beat with an electric beater till creamy.
3. Add the egg and mix well. Add the vanilla essence and mix well.
4. Fold in the flour mixture into it and mix well. Cover with cling film and refrigerate the mixture for half an hour.
5. Preheat the oven to 180°C/350°F/Gas Mark 4.
6. Divide the dough into small portions and roll into balls. Flatten them slightly and arrange them a little apart on a baking tray.
7. Place the tray in the preheated oven and bake for fifteen to twenty minutes or till light golden brown.
8. Cool and store in an airtight container.

Chocolate Éclairs

{ This French pastry is not that hard to make when you have a recipe as excellent as this one. Follow it step by step and present your loved ones with an exotic snack! }

Ingredients

Pastry
¾ cup refined flour (maida)
A pinch of salt
75 grams chilled butter, diced
3 eggs, beaten

Filling
1 cup whipping cream

Chocolate Icing
50 grams dark chocolate
25 grams unsalted butter

Method:

1. Preheat the oven to 200°C/400°F/Gas Mark 6.
2. Sift the flour and salt into a bowl. Place the butter and one cup of water in a non-stick pan and stir over low heat until the butter melts. Add the flour all at once and stir, over medium heat, until the mixture forms a ball and begins to leave the sides of the pan.
3. Transfer the mixture into a bowl and cool slightly. Beat in the eggs, one at a time, until the dough is smooth and shiny.
4. Spoon the mixture into a piping bag with a wide nozzle. Fold down the top of the bag so as to squeeze the dough right to the bottom.
5. Line two flat baking trays with greaseproof paper. Squeeze the mixture into medium-sized sausage shapes, placing them well apart on the baking tray, as the éclairs will double in size while baking. Bake in the preheated oven for about thirty minutes.
6. Remove from the oven when the éclairs are puffed and golden brown and feel hard when tapped. Immediately take each éclair off the baking sheet (they will be very hot, so wear oven gloves) and, with the point of a knife, gently slit the top to let out the steam and to prevent the éclairs from becoming soggy. Transfer onto a wire rack to cool and dry out.
7. For the filling, whip the cream in a small bowl until it is just thick enough to hold its shape. Place it in the refrigerator while you make the chocolate icing.
8. For the chocolate icing, melt chocolate in a double boiler, or in a microwave-safe bowl in the microwave oven on HIGH for one minute. Stir in the butter till well mixed.
9. Fill the inside of each éclair with whipped cream using a piping bag with a small nozzle. Dip the top of each éclair into the chocolate icing. Leave the éclairs on the wire rack until the icing has set. Chill and serve.

Chocolate Coated Nuts

Your hunt for sweet bliss ends here....
crunchy nuts ensconced in creamy chocolate!

Ingredients

½ cup chopped dark chocolate
¼ cup chopped white chocolate
12 almonds
12 cashew nuts

Method:

1. Roast the almonds and cashew nuts in a non-stick pan till light brown. Take the pan off the heat and spread the roasted nuts on a tray to cool.
2. Place the dark chocolate in a microwave-safe bowl and melt in a microwave oven on HIGH for thirty seconds. Take the pan off the heat and allow the chocolate to cool, stirring continuously, to 30°C.
3. Dip the roasted nuts in the melted chocolate. Using a fork, place the nuts on a silicon sheet or butter paper. Refrigerate for fifteen to twenty minutes.
4. Place the white chocolate in a microwave-safe bowl and melt in a microwave oven on HIGH for thirty seconds. Take the pan off the heat and allow the chocolate to cool, stirring continuously, to 30ºC.
5. Pour the melted white chocolate in a piping bag with a pointed nozzle and drizzle an attractive design on the coated nuts. Refrigerate for ten minutes.
6. Serve chilled.

Chocolate Shrewsbury Biscuits

{ Baked with love, presented with great care, ideal biscuits that pack up neatly for gifting! Make your festive occasions memorable... }

Ingredients

½ cup dark chocolate chips
½ cup butter
½ cup + 3 tablespoons caster sugar
2 egg yolks
A few drops of vanilla essence
1½ cups refined flour (maida)
1 teaspoon lemon rind

Method:

1. Beat the butter and caster sugar in a bowl till light and creamy. Add the egg yolks and mix well. Add the vanilla essence and mix well.
2. Sift the flour directly into the butter mixture. Combine gently and knead into a soft dough.
3. Add the lemon rind and mix well. Wrap the dough in cling film and refrigerate for thirty to forty minutes.
4. Preheat the oven to 180°C/350°F/Gas Mark 4.
5. Divide the dough into sixteen equal portions and shape into balls. Sprinkle chocolate chips on each.
6. Flatten the balls lightly on your palm and arrange the cookies on a greased baking tray, keeping sufficient distance between them.
7. Place the tray in the preheated oven and bake for twenty to twenty-five minutes.
8. Remove from oven and let the biscuits cool down to room temperature.
9. Serve or store in an airtight container.

Sugarfree Oats & Chocolate Cookies

{ With a health slant and almost guilt free! }

Ingredients

½ cup chopped unsweetened chocolate
¾ cup oats
¾ cup butter
¼ cup + ⅔ tablespoon sugar substitute (sucralose)
1 egg
1 cup + 2 tablespoons refined flour (maida)
1½ teaspoons baking powder

Method:

1. Preheat the oven to 180°C/350°F/Gas Mark 4. Line a seven-inch by five-inch baking tray with butter paper.
2. Place the butter and sugar substitute (sucralose) in a glass bowl and cream them till light and fluffy. Add the egg and mix well.
3. Sift the flour and baking powder together. Add the oats and chocolate and mix.
4. Add the flour mixture to the butter mixture and mix well.
5. Divide the dough into sixteen equal portions. Make small balls and flatten each lightly on your palm. Place them on the tray, a little distance apart from each other.
6. Place the tray in the preheated oven and bake for twenty to twenty-five minutes.
7. Remove tray from oven and place the cookies on wire rack to cool.
8. Serve when cool or store in an airtight container.

Chocolate Tart

One bite and all your day's woes will disappear like a gentle gust of air!

Ingredients

Tarts
¼ cup + ⅛ cup icing sugar
½ cup butter
½ egg
A few drops of vanilla essence
¾ cup refined flour (maida)
+ for dusting, sifted

Filling
3 tablespoons melted milk chocolate
2 tablespoons white chocolate chips
4 egg yolks
3 tablespoons caster sugar

Method:

1. To make the tarts, mix the icing sugar and butter together in a bowl till light and creamy.
2. Add the egg and mix well. Add the vanilla essence and fold in the flour.
3. Combine gently and knead into a soft dough. Wrap the dough in cling film and refrigerate for thirty minutes.
4. Dust a worktop with a little flour and roll out the dough into a one-eighth-inch thick rectangle.
5. Cut into rounds with a two-and-a-half-inch round cookie cutter. Place these rounds in the tart moulds and refrigerate for twenty minutes.
6. Preheat the oven to 180°C/350°F/Gas Mark 4.
7. Take the moulds out of the refrigerator, trim the edges and prick the base with a fork. Place the moulds in the preheated oven and bake for twenty to twenty-five minutes. Remove from the oven and set aside to cool down to room temperature.
8. To make the filling, boil two cups water in a deep non-stick pan.
9. Place the egg yolks and caster sugar in a bowl and mix well. Place the bowl over the boiling water and cook, whisking continuously, till the mixture thickens and coats the back of a spoon. Take the pan off the heat, set aside till the mixture cools down to room temperature.
10. Add the melted milk chocolate and mix well.
11. Pour this mixture in the prepared tart moulds and serve garnished with white chocolate chips.

Chocolate Macaroons

{ Luxurious tiny treats - for those special moments! }

Ingredients

3 tablespoons unsweetened cocoa powder
A few drops of edible chocolate colour
½ cup ground almonds
3 egg whites
1 cup sugar
½ teaspoon vanilla essence

Method:

1. Preheat the oven to 110°C/225°F/Gas Mark ¼.
2. Sift the ground almonds and cocoa powder together in a bowl.
3. Beat the egg whites until stiff but not dry. Beat in the sugar, a little at a time, until the mixture becomes thick and glossy and forms stiff peaks.
4. Fold in the almond-cocoa mixture, vanilla essence and edible chocolate colour, taking care to fold in one direction only.
5. Pour this mixture into a piping bag and pipe small rounds of three-fourth-inch diameter onto a baking tray lined with a silicon sheet.
6. Place the tray in the preheated oven and bake for forty to forty-five minutes or till crisp.
7. Remove the tray from the oven, cool the macaroons on a wire rack. Sandwich with chocolate truffle and serve.

Chocolate Cream Biscuits

{ A treat of crisp biscuit sandwiched with a creamy and soft chocolate filling... It is best to let the biscuit rest for a while so that the cream sets...but these are so good that we doubt you could keep away from them for long! }

Ingredients

180 grams + 125 grams milk chocolate, chopped
2 tablespoons cocoa powder
3 tablespoons fresh cream
1¼ cups refined flour (maida)
1 teaspoon baking powder
A pinch of salt
100 grams butter
½ cup sugar
2 eggs

Method:

1. Preheat the oven to 170°C/325°F/Gas Mark 3.
2. Sift together the refined flour, baking powder, cocoa powder and salt into a deep bowl.
3. Melt the butter and one hundred and eighty grams milk chocolate in a double boiler and whisk well.
4. Add the sugar to the butter-chocolate mixture and mix well. Add half the sifted ingredients and mix well.
5. Break one egg, add and mix well. Add the remaining sifted ingredients and mix well.
6. Break the remaining egg, add and mix well. Allow to rest for twenty-five to thirty minutes in the refrigerator.
7. Meanwhile, melt one hundred and twenty-five grams milk chocolate in a double boiler. Add the cream and mix well. Remove from heat and let it cool down to room temperature.
8. Place a silicon sheet on a baking tray. Pour chocolate-butter-flour mixture into a piping bag and pipe out twenty small rounds on the sheet.
9. Place the tray in the preheated oven and bake for seven to eight minutes. Remove from oven and let them cool down to room temperature.
10. Pipe a portion of chocolate-cream mixture on ten cookies and cover each of them with another cookie to make a sandwich.
11. Chill in the refrigerator and serve.

Chocolate and Cheese Sandwich

{ Simpler than making the chocolate croissant,
but just as enjoyable to consume!
Everybody loves this sandwich with a twist... }

Ingredients

2 cups grated dark chocolate
1 cup grated processed cheese + for garnishings
12 white bread slices
4 tablespoons butter
2 tablespoons chocolate shavings

Method:

1. Preheat a sandwich grill.
2. Butter all the bread slices on one side. Divide the grated chocolate and grated cheese into eight portions each.
3. Place four slices of bread, buttered side up, on a worktop. Spread one portion each of the chocolate and cheese on the four slices. Cover with four more bread slices, keeping the buttered side up.
4. Spread one portion each of the chocolate and cheese on the bread slices. Cover with the remaining slices, keeping the buttered side up.
5. Place in the sandwich grill, but do not close the lid. Grill till the bottom side is golden and then turn over the sandwich and grill the other side similarly.
6. Remove from grill, place on a serving platter. Sprinkle with chocolate shavings and grated cheese. Serve immediately.

Eggless

Biscotti

Chocolate Almond Biscotti

{ Biscotti, or twice baked biscuits from Italy, are a class apart. Chocolate makes them unforgettable and worth the effort! }

Ingredients

100 grams chocolate chips
100 grams almonds
200 grams egg whites or egg whites of 4½ eggs
180 grams caster sugar
230 grams refined flour (maida)

Method:

1. Preheat the oven to 170°C/325°F/Gas Mark 3.
2. Line a nine-inch by three-and-a half-inch by three-inch loaf tin with butter paper and set aside.
3. Beat the egg whites in a bowl till fluffy. Slowly add the caster sugar and beat till stiff peaks are formed.
4. Sift the flour into another bowl. Add the chocolate chips and almonds and mix well.
5. Add the flour mixture to the beaten egg whites, little by little, and fold in gently. Pour the batter into the prepared mould and place in the preheated oven. Bake for forty to forty-five minutes. Remove from the oven and set aside to cool down to room temperature.
6. Wrap the loaf in a cling film and place in the freezer for six to eight hours.
7. Preheat the oven to 180°C/350°F/Gas Mark 4.
8. Remove the loaf from the freezer and cut one-fourth-inch thick slices and arrange on a baking tray.
9. Place the tray in the preheated oven and bake for four minutes or till light brown. Remove the tray from the oven and set aside to cool.
10. When cool, serve or store in an airtight container.

Chapter 7 >

Desserts

Chocolate Kulfi

{ This is a delicious deviation from the traditional dessert, where creamy nut-strewn kulfi gets a makeover with the dark sweetness of chocolate. }

Ingredients

½ cup grated dark chocolate
1 litre (5 cups) full-cream buffalo milk
5 green cardamoms, crushed
1 tablespoon crushed cashew nuts
1 tablespoon crushed pistachios
1 tablespoon crushed almonds
½ cup condensed milk
1 tablespoon cashew nut paste

Method:

1. Bring the milk to a boil in a deep non-stick pan. Add the crushed green cardamoms and simmer, stirring, for twenty-five to thirty minutes, or till it is reduced to half its original volume.
2. Add the crushed cashew nuts, pistachios and almonds and mix well and continue to simmer.
3. Remove the cardamom skins and continue to simmer for twenty minutes or till the milk is reduced to one-third its original volume.
4. Add the condensed milk and cashew nut paste and mix well. Add the grated chocolate and take the pan off the heat and set aside to cool.
5. Pour into kulfi moulds and keep in the freezer to set for six to eight hours.
6. Unmould and serve.

Walnut Chocolate Fudge

{ The richness of the chocolate fudge also has the welcome crunch of delicious nuts. Go on...have another piece! }

Eggless

Ingredients

1½ cups chopped walnuts
1 tablespoon cocoa powder
Butter, for greasing
1 cup condensed milk
2 tablespoons icing sugar
½ cup grated mawa/khoya
Chocolate Truffle
½ cup chopped dark chocolate
¼ cup fresh cream

Method:

1. To make the chocolate truffle, heat the fresh cream in a small non-stick pan. Take it off the heat and pour it over the chopped chocolate in a bowl. Mix well till the chocolate melts.
   Set aside to cool.
2. Grease a seven-inch by-five-inch rectangular aluminium tray with butter.
3. Pour the condensed milk into another non-stick pan and cook, stirring continuously, till it is light brown in colour.
4. Add the cocoa powder, icing sugar, walnuts, mawa and chocolate truffle. Mix well and cook till the mixture begins to leave the sides of the pan.
5. Transfer this mixture into the tray and let it set at room temperature.
6. Cut into squares and serve.

Chocolate Sauce

{ Pour this warm, thick liquid over anything to make it better! }

Ingredients

4 tablespoons cocoa powder
2 cups milk
½ cup sugar
¼ cup frozen butter,
cut into ½-inch pieces

Eggless

Method:

1. Mix the milk and cocoa powder together in a small non-stick pan.
   Bring it to a boil and simmer, stirring continuously, till it thickens.
2. Add the sugar and continue to cook, stirring continuously.
3. Add the chopped butter and mix well. Serve warm.

Chocolate Ice Cream

{ Who doesn't like chocolate ice cream? Make this recipe and even the few people who will not eat it will be converted! }

Ingredients

¾ cup chopped dark chocolate
½ cup dark chocolate chips
1 cup milk
1 cup milk powder
1¼ cups + 2 tablespoons fresh cream
½ cup powdered sugar

Eggless

Method:

1. Heat one-fourth cup milk in a small non-stick pan and add milk powder to it. Mix well till well blended, ensuring that there are no lumps. Take the pan off the heat and set aside to cool. Place the remaining three-fourth cup milk in the refrigerator to chill.
2. To make chocolate truffle, heat one-fourth cup and two tablespoons fresh cream in another small non-stick pan, but do not boil it. Put the chocolate in a bowl and pour the hot cream over it. Mix well till chocolate melts completely and is well blended. Allow it to cool. Place remaining one cup fresh cream in the refrigerator to chill.
3. Blend the chocolate truffle, milk powder mixture, chilled milk, chilled cream and sugar together till smooth.
4. Pour this mixture into an airtight ice cream container and let it set. When semi set, sprinkle chocolate chips on top and let it set completely.
5. When ready to serve, scoop out into bowls and serve chilled.

Chocolate Coated Fresh Fruits

{ Heart healthy, soul happy – that is what this recipe is all about... Fruit may be healthy, but chocolate sure makes you happy! }

Ingredients

½ medium apple, cut into ½ inch cubes
¼ medium pineapple, cut into ½ inch cubes
2 elaichi bananas, cut into ½ inch thick roundels
½ medium pear, cut into ½ inch cubes
2 cups chopped dark chocolate
¼ cup chopped white chocolate

Method:

1. Melt the dark chocolate in a microwave-safe bowl on microwave HIGH for one minute. Allow it to cool to room temperature, stirring continuously.
2. Pierce toothpicks in the fruit pieces and dip into the melted chocolate.
3. Place the chocolate dipped fruit on butter paper or a silicon sheet. Refrigerate for thirty minutes.
4. Melt the white chocolate in a microwave-safe bowl on microwave HIGH for one minute. Allow it to cool down to room temperature.
5. Pour the melted white chocolate into a piping bag with a thin nozzle and pipe over the fruit pieces, making a zigzag pattern. Refrigerate for ten minutes or more.
6. Serve chilled.

Eggless

Chocolate Pizza

{ Cheese, tomatoes, spices...that is the usual concept of a pizza.
This time, this universal favourite gets a new twist
as it becomes dessert, with cake, fruit, cream and chocolate! }

Ingredients

¾ cup grated white chocolate + ½ cup for garnishing
1 eight-inch round sponge cake
1 cup fresh cream
2 kiwi fruit
8-10 strawberries (or 4-5 plums)
4 tinned pineapple slices

Method:

1. Preheat oven to 190°C/375°F/Gas Mark 5.
2. Cut the sponge cake into half horizontally. Grill both the halves in the preheated oven for three minutes.
3. Heat the fresh cream in a non-stick pan. Place three-fourth cup grated white chocolate in a bowl and add the hot cream and mix till well blended and smooth.
4. Slice the kiwi fruit lengthways. Hull the strawberries and slice neatly. If you are using plums, remove the pips and slice. Slice the pineapple.
5. Remove the sponge slices from the oven and place on a plate. Spread the cream mixture equally and evenly on both the cake halves.
6. Arrange the pineapple slices all round attractively, followed by strawberry (or plum) slices and kiwi slices. Sprinkle the remaining white chocolate on top.
7. Serve immediately.

Eggless

Steamed Chocolate Pudding

{ Steamed food is good for you, they say. Could it get better than this chocolate-steeped dessert? }

Ingredients

1¼ cups chopped white chocolate
½ cup milk
2 tablespoons butter
½ cup condensed milk
½ teaspoon vanilla essence
1 cup fresh white bread crumbs
¼ cup chopped walnuts

Eggless

Method:

1. Boil the milk in a deep non-stick pan. Place the chocolate in a bowl, add the boiling milk and mix well.
2. Put the butter in another bowl, add the condensed milk and vanilla essence and blend till creamy. Add the milk-chocolate mixture and mix well. Add the bread crumbs and walnuts and mix well.
3. Boil sufficient water in a steamer.
4. Pour the prepared batter into silicon cupcake moulds and place in the steamer. Steam on medium heat for thirty minutes.
5. Remove from mould and serve warm.

Chocolate Caramel Custard

{ Chocolate custard is a pudding all children love. Convert it into a more sophisticated flan and adults will be happy too! }

Ingredients

3 tablespoons cocoa powder
2½ cups milk
5 eggs
1½ cups caster sugar
A few drops of vanilla essence

Method:

1. Preheat the oven to 180°C/350°F/Gas Mark 4.
2. Pour the milk into a deep non-stick pan and bring to a boil. Take it off the heat and set aside.
3. Break the eggs into a bowl, add three-fourth quantity of the caster sugar and vanilla essence and beat till well blended.
4. Add the milk slowly to the egg mixture and stir. Add the cocoa powder and mix well.
5. Place the remaining caster sugar in a non-stick pan, add one tablespoon water and heat till the sugar melts and caramelises. Once it becomes light golden in colour, pour it carefully into ramekin moulds and allow it to set.
6. Pour the custard mixture into the moulds. Arrange them in a tray, pour some water in the tray till it reaches half way mark of the moulds and place the tray in the preheated oven. Bake for forty to forty-five minutes.
7. Remove the moulds from the oven and let them cool down to room temperature. Refrigerate for one to two hours.
8. Remove from mould and serve.

Hot Chocolate Nut Sundae

{ Fruit, ice cream, wafer biscuits, nuts and chocolate – does that spell heaven to you? }

Ingredients

¾ cup chocolate sauce
20-25 almonds, roasted and sliced
4 scoops vanilla ice cream
4 scoops fresh strawberry ice cream
4 scoops chocolate ice cream
½ cup black grapes, halved
½ cup green grapes, halved
20-25 fresh strawberries, halved
4 oranges, separated into segments
½ cup pomegranate kernels
4 wafer biscuits, cut into triangles

Method:

1. Select glasses for making the sundae and chill them in a refrigerator.
2. Heat the chocolate sauce in a double boiler. Just before serving, take each glass out of the refrigerator and put a quarter portion of the prepared fruits in it. On it place one scoop each of the three ice creams.
3. Immediately pour one tablespoon of hot chocolate sauce on each. Sprinkle with almonds, decorate with a wafer biscuit and serve immediately.

Eggless

Chapter 8 >

Mithai

Chocolate Chikki

{ Light nougat of rajgira made tastier with a coat of dark chocolate – perfect as dessert at any time! }

Ingredients

1 cup chopped dark chocolate
2 cups rajgira
¾ cup chopped jaggery
1 tablespoon ghee

Eggless

Method:

1. Lightly roast the rajgira in a deep non-stick kadai till fragrant, taking care that the colour does not change. Remove from heat. Grease a clean work top with half tablespoon of ghee.
2. In the same kadai, cook jaggery on medium-low heat till a thick syrup is formed. To test if the syrup is ready put a drop of it in a cup of cold water. If it forms a firm ball the syrup is ready.
3. Add the rajgire and half tablespoon of ghee. Mix and immediately spread on the greased surface. Roll out into one-inch thickness. Ensure that the surface is even. Let it cool slightly. Cut neatly into one-and-half-inch squares.
4. Place the dark chocolate in a microwave-safe bowl and melt in a microwave oven on HIGH for thirty seconds. Take the pan off the heat and allow the chocolate to cool, stirring continuously, to 30°C.
5. Dip a piece of rajgira chikki half way into the melted chocolate. Place it on a silicon sheet till chocolate sets. Serve immediately.

Chocolate Kalakand

{ Kalakand can be intensely sweet and filling. Add chocolate and you will be unable to keep count of how many pieces you have eaten! }

Ingredients

2 tablespoons cocoa powder
2 litres (10 cups) milk
⅛ teaspoon crushed alum
¾ cup sugar
2 tablespoons ghee + for greasing
2 tablespoons liquid glucose
Chocolate shavings, as required

Method:

1. Grease a seven-inch by five-inch rectangular aluminium tray with ghee.
2. Boil the milk in a large non-stick pan on high heat. Add the alum and sugar and continue to cook, stirring continuously, for about an hour or till the milk becomes grainy and thick.
3. Add the ghee and glucose. Mix well and continue to cook till the mixture begins to coat the back of a ladle. Add the cocoa powder and mix well.
4. Transfer the mixture into the greased tray and set aside to cool to room temperature and set.
5. Cut into squares; decorate with chocolate shavings and serve.

Chocolate Burfi

{ The milkiness of Indian sweets is a perfect foil for the dark tint of chocolate. Have a bite and you will want to make this mithai again and again! }

Ingredients

3 tablespoons cocoa powder
500 grams mawa/khoya
Oil for greasing
½-⅓ cup powdered sugar
Silver varq for decorating, optional

Method:

1. Crumble the mawa into fine granules. Grease a seven-inch by five-inch rectangular aluminum tray with oil and set aside.
2. Cook the mawa in a thick-bottomed non-stick pan, stirring continuously, till it melts completely and reaches a thick sauce-like consistency. Take care that it does not change colour.
3. Let it cool slightly and then add the powdered sugar and mix well.
4. Pour half of this mixture into the greased tray. Tap the tray lightly so that the mixture spreads evenly. Set aside to cool to room temperature.
5. Cook the remaining mawa mixture on low heat. Add the cocoa powder and mix well. Take it off the heat when the powder has blended well with the mawa.
6. Pour the chocolate mixture over the white mawa mixture in the tray. Again tap the tray lightly so that the mixture spreads evenly. Set aside to cool completely.
7. Cut into squares or diamonds and serve decorated with silver varq if desired.

Chocolate Peda

{ Tradition gets a twist when chocolate is added to the milky sweet peda made for almost any festival. Try it and make the Gods and your family very happy! }

Ingredients

½ cup grated dark chocolate
2 cups mawa/khoya, crumbled
¼ cup sugar
¼ teaspoon liquid glucose
8 cashew nuts, halved horizontally

Method:

1. Heat a non-stick pan, add the mawa and sauté on low heat, stirring continuously, for fifteen minutes. Transfer into a bowl.
2. Cook the sugar with one-fourth cup water in another non-stick pan on low heat for thirty minutes to make a syrup of one-string consistency. Add the liquid glucose and stir till it blends well.
3. Once the mawa cools slightly, add the syrup and mix well.
4. Melt the chocolate in the microwave on HIGH and whisk till smooth. Add this to the mawa mixture and mix well.
5. When the mixture cools, divide into twelve equal portions and shape into balls. Press lightly and arrange in small paper cups.
6. Decorate with cashew nuts and serve.

Eggless

Chocolate Modak

{ Modaks are usually made for Lord Ganesh. And He will be a very happy deity if you give Him some with chocolate added to the sweet filling! }

Ingredients

¾ cup Basmati rice flour
A pinch of salt
1 teaspoon oil + for greasing
Pure ghee, for serving
Stuffing
½ cup chopped dark chocolate
1½ cups scraped fresh coconut
1 cup grated jaggery
1 tablespoon roasted poppy seeds (khuskhus)
A pinch of green cardamom powder
A pinch of nutmeg powder

Method:

Eggless

1. Heat three-fourth cup of water with salt and one teaspoon oil in a deep non-stick pan.
2. When it comes to a boil, reduce heat and add the rice flour in a steady flow, stirring continuously to prevent lumps from forming. Cover the pan with a deep lid and pour some water into the lid. Cook on low heat for three minutes.
3. Remove the lid, sprinkle some cold water on the rice flour and cover again with the lid with water in it and cook for further three minutes. Repeat this process twice more. Take the pan off the heat and keep it covered for two minutes.
4. Transfer the mixture onto a large plate (parat), grease your palms with oil and knead the dough till smooth and pliable. The dough should not stick to your palms. Rest the dough covered with a damp cloth.
5. To make the stuffing, combine the coconut and jaggery in a non-stick pan and cook on medium heat till most of the moisture dries up. Make sure that you do not overcook the mixture. Add the roasted poppy seeds, cardamom powder and nutmeg powder and mix well. Take the pan off the heat and add chocolate and mix well. Set aside to cool.
6. Divide the coconut mixture into eight equal portions. Divide the dough into eight equal portions and shape them into balls.
7. Grease your fingers and shape each ball into a deep bowl of three-inch diameter. Press the edges to reduce the thickness.
8. Place a portion of the stuffing in the centre, pleat the edges of the dough neatly, sealing them well as you go along. Pinch the top to form a tip.
9. Heat sufficient water in a steamer. Place the modak on a perforated plate, place the plate in the steamer, cover the steamer and steam for ten to twelve minutes.
10. Serve hot modak drizzled with pure ghee.

Chocolate and Nut Karanji

{ Indian celebrations need sweets. To add an unusual touch to the traditional, make chocolate a large part of the filling in these karanji. And make the occasion even more special! }

Ingredients

1½ cups refined flour (maida)
3 tablespoons pure ghee
Oil for deep-frying

Stuffing
½ cup grated dark chocolate
¼ cup chopped almonds
¼ cup chopped walnuts
½ cup grated mawa/khoya
2 tablespoons powdered sugar

Eggless

Method:

1. Put the flour in a deep bowl. Add the ghee and add two to three tablespoons of chilled water or chilled milk. Knead into a medium-soft dough, adding more chilled water or milk as you go along. Divide into small balls and let them rest, covered with a damp cloth.
2. To make the stuffing, mix the mawa, powdered sugar, walnuts, almonds and grated chocolate in a bowl. Chill it in the refrigerator for about ten minutes.
3. Roll out the dough balls into small round puri. Place a puri on the worktop; moisten its edges.
4. Place some stuffing in the centre and fold one side of the puri over the other. Press the edges to seal and further twist the edges with your finger tips in a decorative manner. Or cut the edges with a serrated cutter. You can also make the karanji using a mould.
5. Keep the karanji in the refrigerator for thirty to forty minutes.
6. Heat sufficient oil in a kadai. Deep-fry the karanji, a few at a time, till light brown. Drain on absorbent paper.
7. Serve hot or allow them to cool to room temperature and store in an airtight container.

Note: Since mawa has been used, the shelf life of these karanji is short and therefore they should be consumed fast.

Garnishes

Chocolate Sticks
Chocolate Leaves
Chocolate Flowers
Chocolate Curls
Chocolate Arcs
Chocolate Hearts

Chocolate Arcs

Ingredients: 1 cup chopped dark chocolate

Method

1. Melt the chocolate in a double boiler. Remove from heat and stir well to temper the chocolate till the temperature falls to 30°C.
2. Cut an OHP sheet (see note) into an eight by one-and-a-half-inch piece and place it on a worktop.
3. Pour half the melted chocolate on the OHP sheet and with the help of the spatula spread the chocolate evenly. Continue spreading till it just starts setting. Do not overwork, or else it will have a grainy texture.
4. Remove the excess chocolate from the sides and put it in the chocolate bowl.
5. When the chocolate is still semi-hard hold the OHP sheet in your hand and give it a turn so that both the ends rest on the plate and form an arc shape. Refrigerate for ten minutes.
6. Remove and peel off the OHP sheet carefully. Repeat the procedure for the remaining chocolate.
7. Place the chocolate arcs in an airtight container and place in a refrigerator till further use.

Note: OHP (over head projector) sheets are thin plastic sheets. Flexible and easy to cut with scissors, they are excellent for making decorative shapes with melted chocolate. Also known as transparencies, they are readily available in stationery shops.

Eggless

Chocolate Curls

Ingredients: 1 slab (approx 500 grams) dark chocolate, at room temperature

Method

1. Place the chocolate slab on a worktop.
2. With the help of a ring cutter, scrape the chocolate so that the chocolate scrapes in curls.
3. Cover a tray with cling film and place the prepared chocolate curls on it.
4. Chocolate curls can be used to decorate Eggless Black Forest Gateau.

Note: The narrower side of the chocolate bar helps to create small curls, while the broader side is best to create larger curls.

Eggless

Chocolate Hearts

Ingredients: 1 cup chopped dark chocolate

Method

1. Place an OHP sheet (see note in Chocolate Arcs) on a working surface.
2. Melt the chocolate in a microwave-safe bowl in the microwave on HIGH for one minute. Remove the bowl from the microwave and whisk till the chocolate cools down to 30°C.
3. Pour the melted chocolate into a piping bag, cut the tip to make a very small hole to allow the melted chocolate to pour out easily.
4. Make outlines of heart shapes with the piping bag on the OHP sheets and fill them up with chocolate lines, keeping a small loop empty.
5. Place the sheets in the refrigerator and allow the hearts to set till completely firm.
6. Peel off the hearts gently from the sheets and store them till further use.

Eggless

Chocolate Leaves

Ingredients: 1 cup chopped dark chocolate
A few leaves of mint or carom

Method

1. Melt the chocolate in a microwave safe bowl in the microwave on HIGH for one minute. Remove the bowl from the microwave and whisk well, till the temperature comes down to 30°C.
2. With the help of a brush, apply the melted chocolate on the front side of the leaves and place them on the tray. Refrigerate till the chocolate sets.
3. Remove from refrigerator and carefully peel off the leaves.
4. Store the chocolate leaves in an airtight container and place in a refrigerator till further use.

Eggless

Chocolate Sticks

Ingredients: 1 cup chopped dark chocolate

Method

1. Melt the chocolate in a microwave safe bowl in the microwave on HIGH for one minute. Remove the bowl from the microwave and whisk briskly till the chocolate cools down to 30°C.
2. Pour the chocolate on a silicon sheet and spread evenly with the help of a palate knife.
3. When the chocolate is half set, with the help of a scale and knife, make demarcations of desired width on the chocolate to make the sticks. Refrigerate for ten to fifteen minutes.
4. Peel off the sticks with the help of palate knife and use as required.

Eggless

Chocolate Flowers

Ingredients: 1 cup chopped dark chocolate

Method

1. Melt the chocolate in a microwave-safe bowl in the microwave on HIGH for one minute. Remove the bowl from the microwave and whisk till the chocolate cools down to 30°C.
2. Pour the chocolate on a silicon sheet and spread evenly with the help of a palate knife.
3. When the chocolate is half set, using a flower shaped cutter, make demarcations on the chocolate. Refrigerate for ten to fifteen minutes.
4. Gently remove the flowers with the help of palate knife and use as required.

Eggless

Acknowledgements

Anjali Sawant
Anupa Das
Armaity Motafram
Bharati Joshi
Chef Anil Rohira
Harpal Singh Sokhi
Jaaie Jaiwant
Lata Lohana
Manish Purohit
Neena Murdeshwar
Nisha Dingra
Priyanka Bose
Rahil Aga
Rajeev Matta
Ramya Sarma
Saurabh Mishra
Sheetal Kadam
Swapna Shinde
Urmil Kapoor
Vinitha Ramchandani

Measurements

Ingredients	Quantity/No	Weight
Almonds	10	15 grams
Alum, crushed	1 teaspoon	8 grams
Apple	1 medium	120 grams
Baking powder	1 teaspoon	3 grams
Black grapes	10	40 grams
Brown sugar	1 cup	200 grams
Butter	1 tablespoon	15 grams
Butter	1 cup	150 grams
Butter, melted	1 cup	200 grams
Butterscotch pearls, crushed	1 tablespoon	10 grams
Caramel fudge	1 cup	350 grams
Cashewnut paste	1 tablespoon	15 grams
Cashewnuts	10, 2 1/2 tbsps chopped	20 grams
Castor sugar	1 cup	125 grams
Cheese spread	1 cup	180 grams
Chocolate sauce	1 tablespoon	15 grams
Chocolate truffle	1 tablespoon	12 grams
Cinnamon	1 inch/2.5 cm stick	0.5 gram
Cinnamon powder	1 teaspoon	2 grams
Cocoa powder	1 cup	120 grams
Coconut (freshly scraped)	1 cup	70 grams
Coffee powder	1 teaspoon	5 grams
Condensed milk	1 cup	400 grams
Dark chocolate chips	1 tablespoon	12 grams
Dark chocolate, chopped	1 cup	125 grams
Dark chocolate, grated	1 cup	100 grams
Dark chocolate, melted	1 cup	300 grams
Dessicated coconut	1 cup	150 grams
Egg	1	55-85 grams
Fresh cream	1 cup	200 mls

Ingredients	Quantity/No	Weight
Fresh cream	1 tablespoon	15 mls
Fresh yeast	1 tablespoon	10 grams
Full cream buffalo milk	1 cup	200 mls
Gelatine	1 tablespoon	15 grams
Ghee	1 tablespoon	15 grams
Green cardamom powder	1 teaspoon	2 grams
Green cardamoms	10	3 grams
Honey	1 tablespoon	15 mls
Icecream	1 cup	150 grams
Icing sugar	1 cup	125 grams
Jaggery, grated	1 cup	200 grams
Kiwi	1	120grams
Lemon juice	1 teaspoon	5 mls
Liquid glucose	1 tablespoon	15 grams
Mawa (khoya)	1 cup	180 grams
Milk	1 cup	200 mls
Milk chocolate, chopped	1 cup	125 grams
Milk powder	1 tablespoon	15 grams
Mixed fruit nougat, crushed	1 cup	160 grams
Muesli	1 cup	100 grams
Nutella	1 tablespoon	18 grams
Nutmeg powder	1 teaspoon	4 grams
Oats	1 cup	170 grams
Oil	1 tablespoon	15 mls
Peanut butter	1 tablespoon	20 grams
Peanuts	1 cup	200 grams
Peanuts, roasted	1 cup	120 grams
Pears	1 medium	150 grams
Pineapple	1 slice	50 grams
Pistachios	1/4 cup	30 grams
Pomegranate pearls	1 cup	180 grams
Poppy seeds	1 tablespoon	12.5 grams
Powdered sugar	1 tablespoon	15 grams

Ingredients	Quantity/No	Weight
Puffed rice (Murmura)	1 cup	30 grams
Raisins (white, black)	1 cup	180 grams
Rajgira grains	1 cup	210 grams
Red grapes	10	100 grams
Refined flour (maida)	1 cup	120 grams
Rice crispies	1 cup	50 grams
Rice flour	1 cup	150 grams
Ripe banana, medium	1	120 grams
Ripe mango pulp	1 cup	280 grams
Rum	1 tablespoon	15 mls
Salt	1 teaspoon	5 grams
Soda bicarbonate	1 teaspoon	4 grams
Sponge cake, crumbled	1 cup	125 grams
Star anise	1	2 grams
Strawberry crush	1 tablespoon	15 mls
Sugar	1 tablespoon	15 grams
Sugar	1 cup	250 grams
Tinned cherries, without syrup	1 cup	210 grams
Vanilla essence	1 teaspoon	5 mls
Walnuts	1 cup	120 grams
Whipped cream	1 cup	150 grams
White bread crumbs	1 tablespoon	6 grams
White chocolate chips	1 cup	170 grams
White chocolate, chopped	1 cup	125 grams
White sponge cake	8 inch round	250 grams
Yogurt	1 cup	250 grams

aah! continues...